Virtualization Security

EC-Council | Press

Volume 2 of 2 mapping to

E|CDR™ E|CVT™

EC-Council | Certified DR Professional EC-Council | Certified VT Professional

Certification   Certification

COURSE TECHNOLOGY
CENGAGE Learning™

Australia • Brazil • Japan • Korea • Mexico • Singapore • Spain • United Kingdom • United States

COURSE TECHNOLOGY
CENGAGE Learning™

Virtualization Security
EC-Council | Press

Course Technology/Cengage Learning
  Staff:

Vice President, Career and Professional
  Editorial: Dave Garza

Director of Learning Solutions:
  Matthew Kane

Executive Editor: Stephen Helba

Managing Editor: Marah Bellegarde

Editorial Assistant: Meghan Orvis

Vice President, Career and Professional
  Marketing: Jennifer Ann Baker

Marketing Director: Deborah Yarnell

Marketing Manager: Erin Coffin

Marketing Coordinator: Shanna Gibbs

Production Director: Carolyn Miller

Production Manager: Andrew Crouth

Content Project Manager:
  Brooke Greenhouse

Senior Art Director: Jack Pendleton

EC-Council:

President | EC-Council: Sanjay Bavisi

Sr. Director US | EC-Council:
  Steven Graham

For product information and technology assistance, contact us at
Cengage Learning Customer & Sales Support, 1-800-354-9706

For permission to use material from this text or product,
submit all requests online at **www.cengage.com/permissions**.
Further permissions questions can be e-mailed to
permissionrequest@cengage.com

Library of Congress Control Number: 2010928423

ISBN-13: 978-1-4354-8869-4

ISBN-10: 1-4354-8869-5

Cengage Learning
5 Maxwell Drive
Clifton Park, NY 12065-2919
USA

Cengage Learning is a leading provider of customized learning solutions with office locations around the globe, including Singapore, the United Kingdom, Australia, Mexico, Brazil, and Japan. Locate your local office at: **international.cengage.com/region**

Cengage Learning products are represented in Canada by
Nelson Education, Ltd.

For more learning solutions, please visit our corporate website at **www.cengage.com**

Printed in the United States of America
1 2 3 4 5 6 7 13 12 11 10

Brief Table of Contents

TABLE OF CONTENTS v

PREFACE ix

CHAPTER 1
Introduction to Virtualization **1-1**

CHAPTER 2
VMware ESXi on Linux **2-1**

CHAPTER 3
Microsoft Virtualization **3-1**

CHAPTER 4
Citrix Xen Virtualization **4-1**

CHAPTER 5
Sun Virtualization **5-1**

CHAPTER 6
Red Hat Enterprise Linux Virtualization **6-1**

CHAPTER 7
NoMachine **7-1**

CHAPTER 8
Virtualization Security **8-1**

INDEX **I-1**

Table of Contents

PREFACE ix

CHAPTER 1
Introduction to Virtualization **1-1**

    Objectives 1-1

    Key Terms 1-1

    Introduction to Virtualization 1-2

    Virtualization 1-4
        Virtualization Uses 1-4
        Types of Virtualization 1-5
        Virtualization Techniques 1-9
        Virtualization Security Issues 1-13
        Disaster Recovery Through Virtualization 1-14
        Virtualization Vendors 1-14

    Chapter Summary 1-18

    Review Questions 1-19

    Hands-On Projects 1-20

CHAPTER 2
VMware ESXi on Linux **2-1**

    Objectives 2-1

    Key Terms 2-1

    Introduction to VMware ESXi on Linux 2-1

    VMware and Business Continuity 2-2

    VMware and Disaster Recovery 2-2

    VMware ESX 2-4
        VMware ESX Server System Architecture 2-6
        Installing ESX Server 3i on Linux 2-6
        Configuring ESX Server 3i 2-8

    VMware vSphere 2-9
        VMware vSphere Component Layers 2-9
        VMware vSphere Components 2-10
        Physical Topology of a vSphere Data Center 2-11
        VMware Consolidated Backup 2-12
        Adding a Virtual Machine by Importing a Virtual Appliance 2-12

    VMware vCenter Server 2-13
        vCenter Server Installation 2-14

    Security for ESX Server 3i Systems 2-15
        Recommendations for Securing VMware ESX 2-16

    Chapter Summary 2-16

    Review Questions 2-17

    Hands-On Projects 2-18

CHAPTER 3
Microsoft Virtualization **3-1**

    Objectives 3-1

    Key Terms 3-1

    Introduction to Microsoft Virtualization 3-1

    Virtualization with Hyper-V 3-2
        Key Features of Hyper-V 3-2
        Hyper-V Technology 3-3

Hyper-V Architecture 3-3
Hyper-V in Business Continuity and Disaster Recovery 3-4
Security Assumptions Before Designing a Hyper-V Installation 3-4
Security Goals for Hyper-V 3-5
Installation and Configurations. 3-5
Tips for Hyper-V Security 3-15
Hyper-V Security Best Practices 3-15

Chapter Summary 3-16

Review Questions 3-17

Hands-On Projects 3-18

CHAPTER 4
Citrix Xen Virtualization **4-1**

Objectives 4-1

Key Terms 4-1

Introduction to Citrix Xen Virtualization 4-1

Virtual Server Product Comparison 4-2

Citrix XenServer 5 4-2
XenServer Editions 4-3
XenServer Infrastructure. 4-3
Installing XenServer Host 4-5

XenCenter. 4-7
Configuring the XenCenter Administrator Console 4-7

Xen Security 4-7
Securely Removing Software and Services. 4-8
Limiting Remote Access. 4-9

Citrix XenApp Business Continuity 4-9

Chapter Summary 4-9

Review Questions 4-9

Hands-On Projects 4-10

CHAPTER 5
Sun Virtualization. **5-1**

Objectives 5-1

Key Terms 5-1

Introduction to Sun Virtualization 5-1

Sun Virtualization Features 5-2

Sun Desktop Virtualization 5-3

Sun xVM Ops Center 5-4
Connected and Disconnected Modes of Architecture 5-5
Sun xVM Ops Center Port Requirements 5-5
Enterprise Controller Administration 5-7
xVM Ops Center Installation and Configuration 5-7
Proxy Controller Administration. 5-14
Backup and Recovery. 5-16
User and Role Management. 5-17

Sun xVM VirtualBox 5-18
Features of Sun xVM VirtualBox 5-18
Architecture and Prerequisites of Sun xVM VirtualBox 5-18
VirtualBox Installation on Windows Hosts 5-19
VirtualBox Installation on Mac Hosts 5-19

Sun Virtual Desktop Infrastructure Software. 5-20

Security Concerns with Sun Virtualization 5-20

Chapter Summary 5-21

Review Questions 5-21

Hands-On Projects 5-23

CHAPTER 6
Red Hat Enterprise Linux Virtualization... 6-1

    Objectives 6-1

    Key Terms 6-1

    Introduction to Red Hat Enterprise Linux Virtualization 6-1

    Red Hat Enterprise Linux Virtualization Basics... 6-1

        System Requirements... 6-2

    Installing Red Hat Enterprise Linux Virtualization..................................... 6-3

        Installing Using the yum Command...................................... 6-3

        Creating Guests with virt-manager 6-4

    Installing Guest Operating Systems 6-4

        Installing Red Hat Enterprise Linux 5 as a Paravirtualized Guest 6-4

        Installing a Windows XP Guest.. 6-6

    Configuring Red Hat Enterprise Linux Virtualization.................................. 6-7

        Creating a Virtualized Floppy Disk Controller 6-7

        Adding Storage Devices to Guests 6-7

        Adding a Virtualized CD-ROM or DVD Device to a Guest 6-9

        Configuring Networks and Guests 6-9

        Laptop Network Configuration.. 6-10

    Chapter Summary.. 6-12

    Review Questions 6-12

    Hands-On Projects 6-13

CHAPTER 7
NoMachine 7-1

    Objectives 7-1

    Key Terms 7-1

    Introduction to NoMachine 7-1

    NX Server 7-2

        NX Technology 7-2

        X Window System 7-3

        NX Performance 7-3

        NX Components at Work 7-3

        NX Sessions... 7-3

        NX System Architecture 7-5

        NX Installation and Configuration 7-6

    Chapter Summary.. 7-13

    Review Questions 7-13

    Hands-On Projects 7-14

CHAPTER 8
Virtualization Security 8-1

    Objectives 8-1

    Key Terms 8-1

    Introduction to Virtualization Security 8-1

    Virtualization Security Benefits 8-1

    Virtualization Issues 8-2

        Common Attacks on Virtual Machines.................................... 8-3

        Top Virtualization Security Concerns 8-3

        Virtualization Security Considerations 8-3

    Virtualization Costs 8-3

    Virtualization Security Checklist 8-4

    Chapter Summary.. 8-5

    Review Questions 8-5

    Hands-On Projects 8-6

INDEX **I-1**

Hacking and electronic crimes sophistication has grown at an exponential rate in recent years. In fact, recent reports have indicated that cyber crime already surpasses the illegal drug trade! Unethical hackers better known as *black hats* are preying on information systems of government, corporate, public, and private networks and are constantly testing the security mechanisms of these organizations to the limit with the sole aim of exploiting it and profiting from the exercise. High profile crimes have proven that the traditional approach to computer security is simply not sufficient, even with the strongest perimeter, properly configured defense mechanisms like firewalls, intrusion detection, and prevention systems, strong end-to-end encryption standards, and anti-virus software. Hackers have proven their dedication and ability to systematically penetrate networks all over the world. In some cases *black hats* may be able to execute attacks so flawlessly that they can compromise a system, steal everything of value, and completely erase their tracks in less than 20 minutes!

The EC-Council Press is dedicated to stopping hackers in their tracks.

About EC-Council

The International Council of Electronic Commerce Consultants, better known as EC-Council was founded in late 2001 to address the need for well-educated and certified information security and e-business practitioners. EC-Council is a global, member-based organization comprised of industry and subject matter experts all working together to set the standards and raise the bar in information security certification and education.

EC-Council first developed the *Certified Ethical Hacker,* C|EH program. The goal of this program is to teach the methodologies, tools, and techniques used by hackers. Leveraging the collective knowledge from hundreds of subject matter experts, the C|EH program has rapidly gained popularity around the globe and is now delivered in over 70 countries by over 450 authorized training centers. Over 60,000 information security practitioners have been trained.

C|EH is the benchmark for many government entities and major corporations around the world. Shortly after C|EH was launched, EC-Council developed the *Certified Security Analyst,* E|CSA. The goal of the E|CSA program is to teach groundbreaking analysis methods that must be applied while conducting advanced penetration testing. E|CSA leads to the *Licensed Penetration Tester,* L|PT status. The *Computer Hacking Forensic Investigator,* C|HFI was formed with the same design methodologies above and has become a global standard in certification for computer forensics. EC-Council through its impervious network of professionals, and huge industry following has developed various other programs in information security and e-business. EC-Council Certifications are viewed as the essential certifications needed where standard configuration and security policy courses fall short. Providing a true, hands-on, tactical approach to security, individuals armed with the knowledge disseminated by EC-Council programs are securing networks around the world and beating the hackers at their own game.

About the EC-Council | Press

The EC-Council | Press was formed in late 2008 as a result of a cutting edge partnership between global information security certification leader, EC-Council and leading global academic publisher, Cengage Learning. This partnership marks a revolution in academic textbooks and courses of study in Information Security, Computer Forensics, Disaster Recovery, and End-User Security. By identifying the essential topics and content of EC-Council professional certification programs, and repurposing this world class content to fit academic programs, the EC-Council | Press was formed. The academic community is now able to incorporate this powerful cutting edge content into new and existing Information Security programs. By closing the gap between academic study and professional certification, students and instructors are able to leverage the power of rigorous academic focus and high demand industry certification. The EC-Council | Press is set to revolutionize global information security programs and ultimately create a new breed of practitioners capable of combating the growing epidemic of cybercrime and the rising threat of cyber-war.

Disaster Recovery/Virtualization Security Series

Disaster recovery and business continuity are daunting challenges for any organization. With the rise in the number of threats, attacks, and competitive business landscape, it is important that an organization be prepared and have the ability to withstand a disaster. Using the disaster recovery process, an organization recovers the lost data and gains back the access to the software/hardware so that the performance of the business can return to normal. Virtualization technologies gives the advantage of additional flexibility as well as cost savings while deploying a disaster recovery solution. Virtualization lessens the usage of hardware at a disaster recovery site and makes recovery operations easier.

The *Disaster Recovery/Virtualization Series* introduces methods to identify vulnerabilities and takes appropriate countermeasures to prevent and mitigate failure risks for an organization. This series takes an enterprise-wide approach to developing a disaster recovery plan. Students will learn how to create a secure network by putting policies and procedures in place, and how to restore a network in the event of a disaster. It also provides the networking professional with a foundation in disaster recovery principles. This series explores virtualization products such as VMware, Microsoft Hyper-V, Citrix Xen Server and Client, Sun xVM, HP virtualization, NComputing, NoMachine etc. The series when used in its entirety helps prepare readers to take and succeed on the E|CDR-E|CVT certification exam, Disaster Recovery and Virtualization Technology certification exam from EC-Council. The EC-Council Certified Disaster Recovery and Virtualization Technology professional will have a better understanding of how to setup disaster recovery plans using traditional and virtual technologies to ensure business continuity in the event of a disaster.

Books in Series
- *Disaster Recovery/*1435488709
- *Virtualization Security/*1435488695

Virtualization Security

This book provides an introduction to virtualization security including the types of virtualization, the importance of securing virtualization security and discussions of the various virtualization program offerings.

Chapter Contents

Chapter 1, *Introduction to Virtualization,* explains the concepts of virtualization, including types of virtualization, grid computing, and cloud computing. Chapter 2, *VMware ESXi on Linux,* explains how to use VMware for business continuity budgeting, how to install, configure, use and implement security measures for VMware ESX Server 3i and how to understand the architecture of the VMware ESX server system. Chapter 3, *Microsoft Virtualization,* provides an overview of Microsoft Virtualization including Hyper-V. Chapter 4, *Citrix Xen Virtualization,* discusses how to effectively use Citrix Xen virtualization with the XenServer and XenClient programs. Chapter 5, *Sun Virtualization,* provides an overview of Sun virtualization products and services; how to install, configure and administer xVM Ops Center, how to install VirtualBox for both Windows and Mac hosts and discusses Sun Virtual Desktop Infrastructure Software. Chapter 6, *Red Hat Enterprise Linux Virtualization,* explains how to implement this type of virtualization, how to create a guest operating system and create a virtualized floppy disk controller. Chapter 7, *NoMachine,* explains NX components and how they work; a discussion of NX Client, NX Node, NX Server is also included. Chapter 8, *Virtualization Security,* explains the importance of virtualization security, how to recognize common attacks on virtual machines; and how to secure a virtual server environment.

Chapter Features

Many features are included in each chapter and all are designed to enhance the learner's learning experience. Features include:

- *Objectives* begin each chapter and focus the learner on the most important concepts in the chapter.
- *Key Terms* are designed to familiarize the learner with terms that will be used within the chapter.
- *Chapter Summary*, at the end of each chapter, serves as a review of the key concepts covered in the chapter.

- *Review Questions* allow the learner to test their comprehension of the chapter content.
- *Hands-On Projects* encourage the learner to apply the knowledge they have gained after finishing the chapter Center. Content for this book does not necessarily lend itself to "hands-on" lab activities. We have included additional reading activities to enhance learner knowledge base. Note: you will need your access code provided in your book to enter the site. Visit *www.cengage.com/community/eccouncil* for a link to the Student Resource Center or follow the directions on your access card.

Student Resource Center

The Student Resource Center contains all the files you need to complete the Hands-On Projects found at the end of the chapters. Access the Student Resource Center with the access code provided in your book. Visit *www.cengage.com/community/eccouncil* for a link to the Student Resource Center.

Additional Instructor Resources

Free to all instructors who adopt the *Virtualization Security* book for their courses is a complete package of instructor resources. These resources are available from the Course Technology web site, *www.cengage.com/coursetechnology*, by going to the product page for this book in the online catalog, click on the Companion Site on the Faculty side; click on any of the Instructor Resources in the left navigation and login to access the files. Once you accept the license agreement, the selected files will be displayed.

Resources include:

- *Instructor Manual*: This manual includes course objectives and additional information to help your instruction.
- *ExamView Testbank*: This Windows-based testing software helps instructors design and administer tests and pre-tests. In addition to generating tests that can be printed and administered, this full-featured program has an online testing component that allows students to take tests at the computer and have their exams automatically graded.
- *PowerPoint Presentations*: This book comes with a set of Microsoft PowerPoint slides for each chapter. These slides are meant to be used as a teaching aid for classroom presentations, to be made available to students for chapter review, or to be printed for classroom distribution. Instructors are also at liberty to add their own slides.
- *Labs*: Content for this book does not necessarily lend itself to "hands-on" lab activities. We have included additional reading activities to enhance learner knowledge base.
- *Assessment Activities*: Additional assessment opportunities including discussion questions, writing assignments, internet research activities, and homework assignments along with a final cumulative project.
- *Final Exam*: Provides a comprehensive assessment of *Virtualization Security* content.

Cengage Learning Information Security Community Site

This site was created for learners and instructors to find out about the latest in information security news and technology.

Visit *community.cengage.com/infosec* to:

- Learn what's new in information security through live news feeds, videos and podcasts.
- Connect with your peers and security experts through blogs and forums.
- Browse our online catalog.

How to Become ECDR-ECVT Certified

The EC-Council Disaster Recovery and Virtualization Technology certification will fortify the disaster recovery and virtualization technology knowledge of system administrators, systems engineers, enterprise system architects, hardware engineers, software engineers, technical support individuals, networking professionals, and any IT professional who is concerned about the integrity of the network infrastructure. This is an advanced course for experienced system administrators and system integrators scaling their organization's deployment of the virtualization technologies. The ECDR-ECVT Program certifies individuals and explores installation, configuration, and management of different virtualization products. A certified EC-Council Disaster Recovery and Virtualization Technology professional will better understand how to recover after a disaster so that there is proper business continuity.

To achieve the certification, you must pass the ECDR-ECVT Professional exam 312-55.

E|CDR-E|CVT Certification exam is available through Prometric Prime. To obtain your certification after your training, you must:

1. Purchase an exam voucher from the EC-Council Community Site at Cengage: *www.cengage.com/community/eccouncil.*

2. Speak with your Instructor or Professor about scheduling an exam session, or visit the EC-Council Community Site referenced above for more information.

3. Attempt and pass the E|CDR—E|CVT certification examination with a score of 70% or better.

About our other EC-Council | Press Products

Ethical Hacking and Countermeasures Series

The EC-Council | Press *Ethical Hacking and Countermeasures* series is intended for those studying to become security officers, auditors, security professionals, site administrators, and anyone who is concerned about or responsible for the integrity of the network infrastructure. The series includes a broad base of topics in offensive network security, ethical hacking, as well as network defense and countermeasures. The content of this series is designed to immerse the learner into an interactive environment where they will be shown how to scan, test, hack and secure information systems. A wide variety of tools, viruses, and malware is presented in these books, providing a complete understanding of the tactics and tools used by hackers. By gaining a thorough understanding of how hackers operate, ethical hackers are able to set up strong countermeasures and defensive systems to protect their organization's critical infrastructure and information. The series when used in its entirety helps prepare readers to take and succeed on the C|EH certification exam from EC-Council.

Books in Series
- *Ethical Hacking and Countermeasures: Attack Phases*/143548360X
- *Ethical Hacking and Countermeasures: Threats and Defense Mechanisms*/1435483618
- *Ethical Hacking and Countermeasures: Web Applications and Data Servers*/1435483626
- *Ethical Hacking and Countermeasures: Linux, Macintosh and Mobile Systems*/1435483642
- *Ethical Hacking and Countermeasures: Secure Network Infrastructures*/1435483650

Computer Forensics Series

The EC-Council | Press *Computer Forensics* series, preparing learners for C|HFI certification, is intended for those studying to become police investigators and other law enforcement personnel, defense and military personnel, e-business security professionals, systems administrators, legal professionals, banking, insurance and other professionals, government agencies, and IT managers. The content of this program is designed to expose the learner to the process of detecting attacks and collecting evidence in a forensically sound manner with the intent to report crime and prevent future attacks. Advanced techniques in computer investigation and analysis with interest in generating potential legal evidence are included. In full, this series prepares the learner to identify evidence in computer related crime and abuse cases as well as track the intrusive hacker's path through client system.

Books in Series
- *Computer Forensics: Investigation Procedures and Response*/1435483499
- *Computer Forensics: Investigating Hard Disks, File and Operating Systems*/1435483502
- *Computer Forensics: Investigating Data and Image Files*/1435483510
- *Computer Forensics: Investigating Network Intrusions and Cybercrime*/1435483529
- *Computer Forensics: Investigating Wireless Networks and Devices*/1435483537

Network Defense Series

The EC-Council | Press *Network Defense* series, preparing learners for E|NSA certification, is intended for those studying to become system administrators, network administrators and anyone who is interested in network security technologies. This series is designed to educate learners, from a vendor neutral standpoint, how to defend the networks they manage. This series covers the fundamental skills in evaluating internal and external threats to network security, design, and how to enforce network level security policies, and ultimately protect an organization's information. Covering a broad range of topics from secure network fundamentals, protocols & analysis, standards and policy, hardening infrastructure, to configuring IPS, IDS and firewalls, bastion host and honeypots, among many other topics, learners completing this series will have a full understanding of defensive measures taken to secure their organizations information. The series when used in its entirety helps prepare readers to take and succeed on the E|NSA, Network Security Administrator certification exam from EC-Council.

Books in Series
- *Network Defense: Fundamentals and Protocols*/1435483553
- *Network Defense: Security Policy and Threats*/1435483561
- *Network Defense: Perimeter Defense Mechanisms*/143548357X
- *Network Defense: Securing and Troubleshooting Network Operating Systems*/1435483588
- *Network Defense: Security and Vulnerability Assessment*/1435483596

Penetration Testing Series

The EC-Council | Press *Penetration Testing* series, preparing learners for E|CSA/LPT certification, is intended for those studying to become Network Server Administrators, Firewall Administrators, Security Testers, System Administrators and Risk Assessment professionals. This series covers a broad base of topics in advanced penetration testing and security analysis. The content of this program is designed to expose the learner to groundbreaking methodologies in conducting thorough security analysis, as well as advanced penetration testing techniques. Armed with the knowledge from the Security Analyst series, learners will be able to perform the intensive assessments required to effectively identify and mitigate risks to the security of the organization's infrastructure. The series when used in its entirety helps prepare readers to take and succeed on the E|CSA, Certified Security Analyst certification exam.

Books in Series
- *Penetration Testing: Security Analysis*/1435483669
- *Penetration Testing: Procedures and Methodologies*/1435483677
- *Penetration Testing: Network and Perimeter Testing*/1435483685
- *Penetration Testing: Communication Media Testing*/1435483693
- *Penetration Testing: Network Threat Testing*/1435483707

Cyber Safety/1435483715

Cyber Safety is designed for anyone who is interested in learning computer networking and security basics. This product provides information cyber crime; security procedures; how to recognize security threats and attacks, incident response, and how to secure internet access. This book gives individuals the basic security literacy skills to begin high-end IT programs. The book also prepares readers to take and succeed on the Security|5 certification exam from EC-Council.

Wireless Safety/1435483766

Wireless Safety introduces the learner to the basics of wireless technologies and its practical adaptation. *Wireless|5* is tailored to cater to any individual's desire to learn more about wireless technology. It requires no pre-requisite knowledge and aims to educate the learner in simple applications of these technologies. Topics include wireless signal propagation, IEEE and ETSI Wireless Standards, WLANs and Operation, Wireless Protocols and Communication Languages, Wireless Devices, and Wireless Security Network. The book also prepares readers to take and succeed on the Wireless|5 certification exam from EC-Council.

Network Safety/1435483774

Network Safety provides the basic core knowledge on how infrastructure enables a working environment. Intended for those in an office environment and for the home user who wants to optimize resource utilization, share infrastructure and make the best of technology and the convenience it offers. Topics include foundations of networks, networking components, wireless networks, basic hardware components, the networking environment and connectivity as well as troubleshooting. The book also prepares readers to take and succeed on the Network|5 certification exam from EC-Council.

Acknowledgements

Michael H. Goldner is the Chair of the School of Information Technology for ITT Technical Institute in Norfolk Virginia, and also teaches bachelor level courses in computer network and information security systems. Michael has served on and chaired ITT Educational Services Inc. National Curriculum Committee on Information Security. He received his Juris Doctorate from Stetson University College of Law, his undergraduate degree from Miami University and has been working over fifteen years in the area of Information Technology. He is an active member of the American Bar Association, and has served on that organization's Cyber Law committee. He is a member of IEEE, ACM and ISSA, and is the holder of a number of industrially recognized certifications including, CISSP, CEH, CHFI, CEI, MCT, MCSE/Security, Security+, Network+ and A+. Michael recently completed the design and creation of a computer forensic program for ITT Technical Institute, and has worked closely with both EC-Council and Delmar/Cengage Learning in the creation of this EC-Council Press series.

## Chapter 1

Introduction to Virtualization

Objectives

After completing this chapter, you should be able to:

- Define virtualization
- Explain the purpose of virtualization
- List the types of virtualization
- List system virtualization techniques
- Name the benefits of virtualization in the data center
- Explain grid computing
- Define software as a service (SaaS)
- Explain cloud computing
- List security vulnerabilities involved with virtualization
- Name prominent virtualization vendors

Key Terms

Application virtualization   the process of running software from a remote server

Cloud computing   a computing paradigm in which tasks are assigned to a combination of connections, software, and services accessed over a network

Clustering   a technique involving using multiple computers (PCs or UNIX workstations), multiple storage devices, and redundant interconnections to create a single available system

Desktop virtualization   a type of virtualization that uses virtual machines to allow multiple network subscribers to maintain individualized desktops on a centrally located computer

Grid computing   the process of applying the resources of many computers in a network to a single problem at the same time

Migration   the process of moving data, applications, operating systems, and processes from one machine to another

Network virtualization   a method of combining the available resources in a network by splitting up the available bandwidth into channels to particular servers or devices in real time

Paravirtualization   a process that provides partial simulation of the underlying hardware

Server sprawl   a situation in which multiple underutilized servers take up space and consume a large amount of resources

Server virtualization   a type of virtualization that masks the server's resources, including the number and identities of the individual physical servers, processors, and operating systems, from server users

Software as a service (SaaS)   a software deployment model in which an application is licensed for use as a service and provided to customers on demand

Storage virtualization   the pooling of physical storage from multiple network storage devices into what appears to be a single storage device that is managed from a central console

Virtualization   a framework or methodology that divides the resources of a computer into multiple execution environments

Introduction to Virtualization

Virtualization (Figure 1-1) is a framework or methodology that divides the resources of a computer into multiple execution environments. The resources are divided by applying one or more concepts or technologies, such as hardware and software partitioning, time-sharing, partial or complete machine simulation, or emulation. Virtualization has changed the way that hardware and software are used. Before virtualization, a single operating system's image was used for every machine, as shown in Figure 1-2. This required a great deal of capital to pay for hardware, software, and overall infrastructure. Running multiple applications on a single machine can create conflicts and leads to underutilization of a network's potential.

Virtualization has made the hardware independent from the applications as well as the operating system. The virtualization process occurs when a virtualization layer is formed in order to isolate one application/OS from another one, as shown in Figure 1-3. It manages applications and machines as a single unit by encapsulating them into a single virtual machine. Virtualization is flexible, scalable, and helps during disaster recovery.

Virtualization emerged with the concept of time-sharing. IBM first introduced the concept in the 1960s to partition large mainframe hardware to enhance hardware utilization. It was implemented to logically partition the mainframe computers into separate virtual machines.

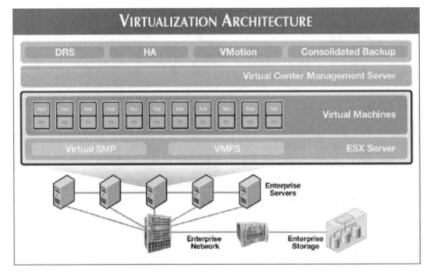

Figure 1-1   Virtualization divides a computer's resources into multiple execution environments.

Types of Virtualization

Various types of virtualization are used, depending on the needs of an organization. Virtualization is classified into the following types:

- Desktop virtualization
- Server virtualization
- Storage virtualization
- Network virtualization
- Application virtualization

Desktop Virtualization

Desktop virtualization (Figure 1-5) uses virtual machines to allow multiple network subscribers to maintain individualized desktop operating systems on a single computer. In desktop virtualization, the users are connected to one central machine, with LAN/WAN/Internet as a medium that allows the client to access all the applications and other resources within a virtual environment without connecting to the specific hardware.

Desktop virtualization is more efficient than traditional systems in which every computer operates as an individual unit with its own operating system and resources. Figure 1-6 shows an example of desktop virtualization architecture.

Desktop virtualization includes the following features:

- Provides a reduction in the cost of deploying new applications
- Runs on multiple operating systems (same or different) as per the user's requirements
- Has almost zero downtime when a hardware failure occurs
- Provides the ability to access the enterprise desktop environment from any system
- Manages many machines
- Can share and allocate resources to multiple users
- Provides integrity to the user's information

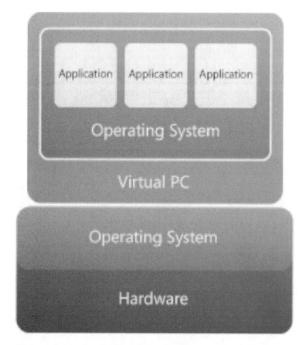

Figure 1-5 Desktop virtualization uses virtual machines to allow multiple network subscribers to maintain individualized desktops on a centrally located computer.

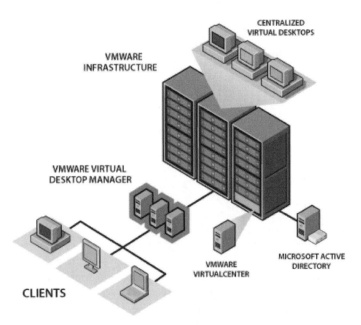

Figure 1-6 Desktop virtualization allows multiple clients to use one application.

Server Virtualization

Server virtualization (Figure 1-7) is the masking of the server's resources, including the number and identities of the individual physical servers, processors, and operating systems, from server users. It is the most commonly used type of virtualization. It can be implemented on all CPU platforms and architectures. The following three approaches are used to implement server virtualization:

1. The virtual machine model
2. The paravirtual machine model
3. Virtualization at the operating system (OS) layer

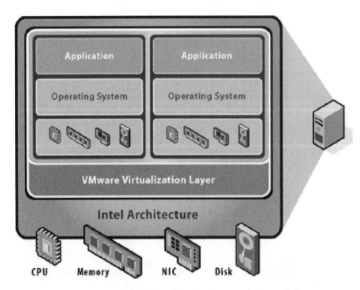

Figure 1-7 Server virtualization is the masking of the server's resources, including the number and identities of the individual physical servers, processors, and operating systems, from server users.

Server virtualization accomplishes the following tasks:

- Reduces the number of physical servers
- Implements the server consolidation strategy, which increases the efficiency of the data center
- Does not affect other applications if one application shuts down or there is a problem with an application

Server Sprawl Server virtualization offers a solution to server sprawl. ***Server sprawl*** is a situation in which multiple underutilized servers take up space and consume a large amount of resources. In this situation, only a maximum of 20%–30% of the physical server's capabilities are used.

The following issues are a result of server sprawl:

- Complexity in the administration; this affects the following areas:
  - Patch management
  - Disaster recovery
  - Backup
  - Server management
  - Troubleshooting
- Increase in hardware cost

Causes of server sprawl include the following:

- Purchase of a large number of inexpensive assets
- Low-end servers
- The practice of dedicating servers to single applications

Storage Virtualization

Storage virtualization (Figure 1-8) is the pooling of physical storage from multiple network storage devices into what appears to be a single storage device that is managed from a central console. This type of virtualization is commonly used in a storage area network (SAN). It provides for the backup, archiving, and recovery of data and applications in a short amount of time. It is hardware independent and uses heterogeneous storage devices. Storage virtualization provides the following benefits:

- Offers security with the ability to hide data from unauthorized servers
- Provides the ability to edit information to meet the needs of individual servers
- Meets the user's storage requirements and simplifies the system's administration
- Offers easy data migration, replication, and storage aggregation
- Provides disaster recovery, which maintains business continuity

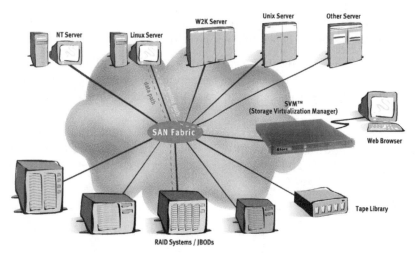

Figure 1-8 Storage virtualization is the pooling of physical storage from multiple network storage devices into what appears to be a single storage device that is managed from a central console.

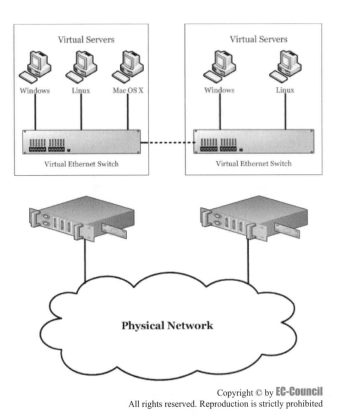

Figure 1-9 Network virtualization is a method of combining the available resources in a network by splitting up the available bandwidth into channels to a particular server or device in real time.

Network Virtualization

Network virtualization (Figure 1-9) is a method of combining the available resources in a network by splitting up the available bandwidth into channels to particular servers or devices in real time. It offers a way to run multiple networks in which each is customized for a particular purpose. In network virtualization, the multiple networks work simultaneously over a shared substrate. It optimizes the network speed and thus offers reliability, flexibility, scalability, and security.

Network virtualization is effective in networks that experience sudden, large, and unforeseen surges in usage. It can be either internal or external, depending upon the implementation provided by vendors.

- *Internal network virtualization*: In an internal network virtualization, a system is configured with containers, such as the Xen Domain, and combined with hypervisor control programs, such as the VNIC, in order to create a "network in a box." This improves the overall efficiency of the system.

- *External network virtualization*: In an external network virtualization, one or more local networks are combined or divided into virtual networks. The main idea behind this virtualization is to enhance the efficiency of a data center or an organization's network. The components that make this possible are the VLAN and the virtual switch.

Application Virtualization

Application virtualization is the process of running software from a remote server. It is used to accomplish the following tasks:

- Avoiding installing applications on the client's system
- Offering negligible application conflicts

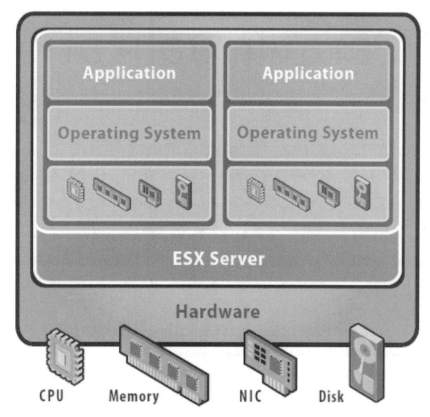

Figure 1-10   Full virtualization is a technique that provides a complete simulation of the underlying hardware.

- Avoiding the need for testing
- Making it possible to run different versions of the same application simultaneously
- Providing support for Web, client-server, and server-based computing applications

Application virtualization creates the following benefits:

- Reduces cost for hardware, software, and OS licenses
- Provides the ability to share the workload
- Makes it easier to manage, upgrade, and migrate applications
- Maximizes the utilization of existing resources
- Offers manageability, portability, encapsulation, and compatibility of applications

Virtualization Techniques

Full Virtualization

Full virtualization (Figure 1-10) is a technique that provides a complete simulation of the underlying hardware. It has a wide range of support for the guest operating system. Operating systems can be installed without any modification. It offers complete isolation of each virtual machine.

Full virtualization includes the following benefits:

- Allows for sharing a computer among multiple users
- Isolates one user from another in terms of program control
- Emulates new hardware in order to achieve security, productivity, and reliability

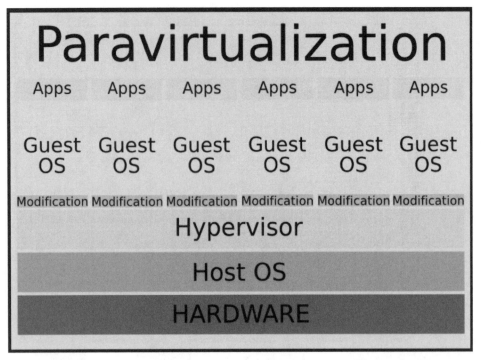

Figure 1-11 Paravirtualization is a process that provides partial simulation of the underlying hardware.

Paravirtualization

Paravirtualization (Figure 1-11) is a process that provides partial simulation of the underlying hardware. It provides a specific address space for each virtual machine. Though it is complex to implement, it is easier to implement than full virtualization.

Paravirtualization allows the virtual machine monitor (VMM) to be simpler. It also allows the virtual machines to achieve performance closer to the nonvirtualized hardware, and when no hardware assistance is provided, paravirtualized guests tend to be the highest-performing VMs for disks as well as for disk I/O.

Hosted and Bare-Metal Virtualization

Hosted and bare-metal virtualization technologies are two common approaches to virtualization. Hosted virtualization provides services on top of a standard operating system. In bare-metal virtualizaton, the user can interface directly with the computer hardware, without a host operating system.

Partitioning

Partitioning makes a physical resource appear as multiple virtual resources. This solution is available with VMware, Xen, and Virtual Iron. Partitioning allows for the following configurations:

- A cluster of machines into subclusters
- A machine into multiple subsets on physical boundaries
- One or more processors and other resources into multiple virtual machines supporting different operating systems
- Operating system into different containers
- Resources managed by an operating system between different applications
- Resources of a JVM between different Java applications

Migration

Migration is the process of moving data, applications, operating systems, and processes from one machine to another. Migration takes the following forms:

- *Data migration*: Data migration is the process of moving data between storage types, formats, or computer systems.

- *Process migration*: Process migration involves moving processes from one machine to another.

- *System migration*: System migration is the process of moving a set of instructions or programs from one platform to another for compatibility.

Clustering

Clustering is using multiple computers (PCs or UNIX workstations), multiple storage devices, and redundant interconnections to create a single available system. This technique links one or more systems into a network for the advantage of parallel processing.

Clusters come in the following forms:

- High-availability clusters
- Load-balancing clusters
- High-performance clusters

Clusters provide the following improvements:

- Increased processing power (parallel processing)
- Improved network technology, scalability, and availability

Virtualization and Clustering

Virtualization and clustering are techniques used for disaster recovery. Virtualization and clustering are two different technologies with different objectives, but they both serve the needs of the data center.

Virtualization is a strategy for high utilization, reduced management, and business agility, whereas clustering is a strategy for high-performance computing, load balancing, and increased application availability. Both technologies are used at the application level and are specific to one application.

Data center managers use technologies such as VMware, Xen, and user-mode Linux to build servers with distinct partitions that are independent and receive a slice of server resources, allowing for better utilization of server resources by 15% compared to that of single-purpose servers. This avoids the built-in wastes and high operational costs of installing many underutilized servers.

Clustering is specific to single applications, as seen with Oracle's RAC, and is done at the application level. To support clustering, data center managers should make use of two distinct infrastructures, either fractional servers or aggregates of servers.

Benefits of Virtualization in the Data Center

Virtualization provides the following benefits for the data center:

- *High availability and disaster recovery*: Virtualization provides an instant failover plan that provides business continuity throughout disruptive events.

- *Decreased deployment times*: Unlike the physical installation of server hardware, a virtual machine requires simple configuration.

- *Platform standardization*: Virtualization platforms decouple the link between the operating system and physical hardware. This allows resources to be moved between the physical servers with little or no reconfiguration.

- *Level of service*: It offers sharing of workloads and thus provides built-in application redundancy.

- *Legacy applications*: It supports older applications, though their use is negligible.

- *Security*:

  - Deployment offers a simplified virtual server provisioning process and ensures the rapid deployment of new systems.

Figure 1-12   Grid computing (or the use of a computational grid) is applying the resources of many computers in a network to a single problem at the same time.

- Isolation limits the security exposure between the virtual machines.
- Rollback helps in recovering from security breaches.
- Abstraction offers only limited direct access to the hardware and physical networks.
- Portability provides backup and disaster recovery of information.

Grid Computing

Grid computing (or the use of a computational grid) is applying the resources of many computers in a network to a single problem at the same time, as shown in Figure 1-12. It can divide and farm out pieces of a program to several thousands of computers. Grid computing is a form of distributed computing in which a super and virtual computer are composed of a cluster of networked, loosely coupled computers acting together to perform complex tasks.

Grid computing services depend on Open Grid Services Architecture (OGSA). OGSA is a set of standards and protocols that enables communication across heterogeneous and geographically dispersed environments.

Grid computing provides the following benefits:

- Enables collaboration and promotes operational flexibility
- Efficiently scales to meet variable business demands
- Increases productivity
- Leverages the existing capital investment

Software as a Service (SaaS)

Software as a service (SaaS) is a software deployment model in which an application is licensed for use as a service and provided to customers on demand. It manages application access, including security, availability, and performance factors.

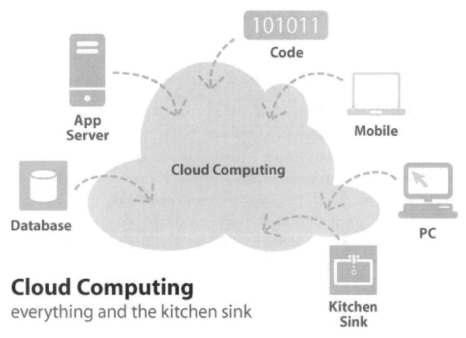

Figure 1-13   Cloud computing is a computing paradigm in which tasks are assigned to a combination of connections, software, and services accessed over a network.

SaaS includes the following features:

- Network-based access
- Centralized management of data using the Internet
- Centralized updating for downloading patches and upgrades

Software as a service offers a multitenant architecture in which all individuals and applications share a single, centrally maintained infrastructure. It offers ease in customization and in accessing applications.

Cloud Computing

A cloud is a virtual server pool used to provide different service profiles at a user's request. *Cloud computing* (Figure 1-13) is a computing paradigm in which tasks are assigned to a combination of connections, software, and services accessed over a network. In cloud computing, data and services reside in scalable data centers that can be globally accessed from any connected devices over the Internet.

Cloud computing provides services on virtual machines allocated on top of a large physical machine pool. It is a platform for computing and storage that allows the user to use resources available on the cloud. Cloud computing offers the following benefits:

- Accessible to all Internet-accessible devices
- Offers e-business, image processing, and log analysis
- Easily accessible in a virtual environment

Virtualization Security Issues

Though virtualization is one of the most widely used technologies in the world, there are several security issues related to it. Virtualization has the following security issues:

- The virtual layer/environment is complex; thus, handling its security issues is complex.
- Virtual machine sprawl can yield security issues for new virtual machines.
- Migrating a virtual machine from one physical server to another may create vulnerabilities for the physical host.

- Both physical host and virtual host security make the virtual environment's security complex.
- Managing a virtual machine's OS patch level is critical.
- Traditional security such as intrusion detection is not applicable to virtual servers.
- Data can be compromised while being shared between virtual and physical servers.

Avoiding Security Threats

The following practices help prevent security threats:

- Always update the virtualization and security software.
- Limit the use of VMs to critical staff.
- Acceptable-use policy should be updated by organizations using virtualization.
- Ensure the use of security products that support virtualization.
- Have well-defined and documented security policies persistently attached and enforced for all VMs as they are migrated, rolled back, or paused and restarted.
- Use segmentation on the physical VM servers.
- Make regular backups.
- Harden virtualization add-on services.

Security Benefits of Virtualization

Virtualization provides the following security benefits:

- Centralized storage environment prevents the loss of critical data when a device is lost, attacked, or stolen. The client devices have no data stored on them. All the data is in centralized storage, which is backed up frequently.
- Isolation of applications means that only one application is affected by a security breach.
- A virtual environment provides the flexibility to share systems without sharing critical information.
- Virtualization provides an extra layer of defense from attacks.

Disaster Recovery Through Virtualization

Virtualization provides the following useful aids to disaster recovery:

- Provides redundant storage for the virtual machines in data centers
- Allows for the easy migration of software, which benefits business continuity
- Decreases the amount of hardware required at a disaster recovery site
- Duplicates a critical server in order to avoid the cost of replacing hardware during the disaster recovery process
- Offers automatic data synchronization
- Allows users to go back to work faster after a hardware failure
- Encapsulates all VMs into single files and restores them with reduced downtime
- Increases business agility

Virtualization Vendors

Virtualization is in high demand due to its advantages and is provided by a large number of vendors. The following vendors are well known for their virtualization products:

- VMware
- Microsoft
- Xen
- Citrix
- Virtual Iron

- Sun
- HP
- NoMachine
- Red Hat
- NComputing
- Parallels

VMware

VMware is one of the leading companies providing virtual products and solutions. It offers a wide range of virtualization products, from free software for virtualizing desktops and servers to comprehensive enterprise-class platforms for optimizing data centers and IT infrastructure.

VMware makes the following products:

- VMware server and data center products
  - *VMware Infrastructure*: This is a virtual data center operating system that unifies the discrete hardware resources to create a shared dynamic platform, while delivering built-in availability, security, and scalability to applications. It is a self-optimizing infrastructure that reduces downtime, increases reliability with disaster recovery, and maximizes the usage of resources.
  - *VMware vCenter Server*: Formerly known as VMware Virtual Center, this manages, automates, and optimizes IT infrastructure. It simplifies IT operations, making the virtual environment easy to administer and control.
  - *VMware ESXi*: This tool runs all production applications with advanced performance on the OS-independent VMware hypervisor.
  - *VMware Server*: This is a hosted virtualization platform that installs like an application on any existing server hardware and partitions a physical server into multiple virtual machines.
  - *VMware vCenter Lab Manager*: This tool gives users on-demand access to the system configurations they need, while achieving significant savings through reduced server, storage, and provisioning costs.
  - *VMware vCenter Site Recovery Manager*: This recovery manager eliminates complex manual recovery steps.
- VMware desktop products
  - *VMware View*: VMware View allows administrators to manage all the desktops on the network from the data center.
  - *VMware Workstation*: This tool maximizes the utilization of desktop systems, allowing users to run multiple operating systems at the same time on a virtual platform.
  - *VMware Player*: This free tool is similar to Workstation in that it allows users to run multiple operating systems at the same time within a virtual platform on a single physical computer.
  - *VMware Fusion*: This program is designed for Mac desktops. It runs Windows applications side-by-side with Mac applications.
  - *VMware ThinApp*: This tool uses application virtualization to eliminate conflicts in deployed applications.
  - *VMware ACE*: VMware ACE controls virtual desktops across an enterprise. It combines the power and versatility of VMs with the security and control of centrally managed computers.

Microsoft Virtualization

Microsoft offers a suite of technologies used to enable an integrated, end-to-end, and virtualized infrastructure. Microsoft offers products in the following fields of virtualization:

- Server virtualization
- Desktop virtualization
- Application virtualization
- Virtualization management

Citrix

Citrix is an application delivery infrastructure system that transforms IT into an on-demand service by centralizing the management and delivery of applications and desktops. It simplifies IT operations by managing a single image of applications, desktops, and servers; accelerating application rollouts; and reducing IT operating costs up to 50%.

VMware Versus Microsoft Versus Citrix, 2009

Figure 1-14 shows a comparison of the virtualization offerings of VMware, Microsoft, and Citrix in 2009.

Sun

Sun offers a broad range of open, scalable virtualization products and services. It offers the following products related to virtualization:

- Desktop virtualization products and services
  - Sun Virtual Desktop Infrastructure (VDI) software
  - Managed Virtual Desktop solution
  - Sun xVM VirtualBox
- Server virtualization products and services
  - Sun xVM Server
  - Solaris containers

	VMware	Microsoft	Citrix's Xen
URL	Vmware.com	Microsoft.com/hyperV	Xensource.com
Free hypervisor product	ESXi	HyperV Server	Xen Server Express
Paid hypervisor products	ESX	(None)	Xen Server Enterprise, Platinum
Guest OS's supported	Windows, Mac, Linux, others	Mostly Windows Family + SUSE	Windows, Linux
Management tools	vCenter Server VMotion vCenter Lab Manager vCenter Converter Infrastructure	System Center VM Manager	Included in paid versions
Advantage	• Widest selection of prebuilt appliances • Widest selection of guest OS support	• HyperV is included as part of Windows Server 2008 64-bit version • Cost-effective licensing of guest Windows VMs	• Open-source solution • Essentials also manages HyperV • 32-CPU support • P2V included in overall solution
Disadvantage	Confusing array of pricing and configuration options	Limited management tools	No prebuilt appliances

Figure 1-14 VMware, Microsoft, and Citrix offer similar virtualization products.

- Sun Fire x64 Servers
- Sun CoolThreads Servers
- Sun Blade modular systems
- Sun SPARC enterprise servers
- LDoms
- Storage virtualization products and services
  - Primary/disk storage
  - Tape storage
  - Storage virtualization services
  - Solaris operating system

HP

The HP Virtual Server Environment (VSE) helps users optimize the server's utilization in real time. It provides an automated virtual infrastructure that can adapt quickly. VSE provides the following features:

- Detailed analysis of large-scale consolidations
- Quick deployment of new services and online applications
- Balanced supply and demand based on business priorities
- Reduction in costs

HP also provides hardware that combines with other vendors such as VMware and Citrix in order to give improvised solutions in a virtual environment.

Red Hat Enterprise Linux Virtualization

Red Hat Enterprise Linux Virtualization provides a platform for open-source computing. Red Hat offers the following virtualization products:

- Server virtualization
  - Red Hat Enterprise Linux 5 Server
  - Red Hat Enterprise Linux 5 Advanced Platform
  - Red Hat Enterprise Linux 5 for Mainframes
- Desktop virtualization
  - Red Hat Enterprise Linux 5 Desktop

Virtual Iron

Virtual Iron is a provider of server virtualization. It offers development and test optimization, and disaster recovery services. It provides true server virtualization, including intelligent virtual machine mobility, high availability, rapid recovery, and performance load balancing. Virtual Iron is able to perform the following tasks:

- Achieve server consolidation
- Simplify server management
- Improve application development and testing
- Achieve business continuity
- Reduce power
- Implement a virtual desktop infrastructure

NoMachine

NoMachine NX is an enterprise-class solution for secure remote access, desktop virtualization, and hosted desktop deployment built around the self-designed and self-developed NX suite of components. NoMachine offers the following products:

- NX Enterprise Desktop
- NX Small Business Server

- NX Enterprise Server
- NX Advanced Server
- NX Server Manager
- NX Web Companion
- NX Client
- NX Builder

Parallels

Parallels offers virtualization exclusively for the Macintosh operating system. It provides virtualization and automation software for consumers, businesses, and service providers for optimized computing. Parallels offers the following virtualization products:

- Desktop virtualization
  - *Parallels Desktop 4.0 for Mac*: This provides the complete suite of essentials to run Windows on a Mac.
  - *Parallels Workstation*: This is an easy-to-use workstation that allows the user to run Windows, Linux, and other operating systems on a single machine without rebooting.
- Server virtualization
  - *Parallels Server for Mac*: This server enables organizations to virtualize the Leopard Server and run virtually any application on Mac servers.
  - *Parallels Server*: This is a bare-metal hypervisor that helps organizations to reduce the costs and complexities of IT infrastructures.
  - *Parallels Virtuozzo Containers 4.0*: This is an OS virtualization solution for Windows and Linux. It creates isolated containers on a single physical server and OS instance.
  - *Parallels Infrastructure Manager (PIM)*: This is an optional add-on Web-based tool for Virtuozzo administrators to perform management of virtualized IT infrastructures.

Chapter Summary

- Virtualization is a framework or methodology that divides the resources of a computer into multiple execution environments. The resources are divided by applying one or more concepts or technologies, such as hardware and software partitioning, time-sharing, partial or complete machine simulation, or emulation.
- Virtualization maximizes the utilization of resources, optimizes IT infrastructure costs, and offers a high level of security.
- Server virtualization allows the user to run multiple guest computers on a single host computer with those guest computers believing they are running on their own hardware.
- Virtualization is a strategy for high utilization, reduced management, and business agility, whereas clustering is a strategy for high-performance computing, load balancing, and increased application availability.
- Migrating a virtual machine from one physical server to another may create vulnerabilities for the physical host.
- A centralized storage environment prevents the loss of critical data when a device is lost, attacked, or stolen. The client devices have no data stored on them. All the data is in centralized storage, which is backed up frequently.

Review Questions

1. Define virtualization.

   _____

   _____

   _____

   _____

2. List the advantages of virtualization.

   _____

   _____

   _____

   _____

3. Discuss the various types of virtualization.

   _____

   _____

   _____

   _____

4. What is desktop virtualization? Discuss the benefits of desktop virtualization.

   _____

   _____

   _____

   _____

5. Discuss various system virtualization techniques.

   _____

   _____

   _____

   _____

6. Discuss the benefits of virtualization in data centers.

   _____

   _____

   _____

   _____

7. What is grid computing?

   _____

   _____

   _____

   _____

8. List the factors to be considered to avoid security threats.

   _____

   _____

   _____

   _____

9. Discuss the security benefits of virtualization.

_____

_____

_____

_____

10. List the various virtualization vendors and their major products.

_____

_____

_____

_____

Hands-On Projects

1. Navigate to Chapter 1 of the Student Resource Center. Open (Types of Virtualization Types of virtualization)Lec05.pdf and read the following topics:

   - Types of Virtualization
   - Code and Process Migration

2. Navigate to Chapter 1 of the Student Resource Center. Open 2006.02.03-figueiredo.pdf and read the following topics:

   - Virtual Computer
   - Virtual Machines
   - Why Virtual Computers?

3. Navigate to Chapter 1 of the Student Resource Center. Open 2008-10.pdf and read the following topics:

   - Scope of Virtualization Services
   - Virtualization Evolution
   - Business Continuity is the Objective

4. Navigate to Chapter 1 of the Student Resource Center. Open True_Cost_Virtual_Server_Solutions.pdf and read the following topics:

   - Charge of the Hypervisors
   - Cost Per App: Why VM Density Matters
   - Testing Density: Not All Hypervisors – or Virtual Infrastructures – are the Same

## Chapter 2

VMware ESXi on Linux

Objectives

After completing this chapter, you should be able to:

- Use VMware software for business continuity and disaster recovery
- Understand VMware ESX Server architecture
- Install, configure, and use VMware ESX Server 3i
- Implement security measures for VMware ESX Server 3i

Key Terms

Standalone host   a computing server in a virtualized environment

Virtual machine   a software implementation of a computer that executes programs as if it were a real, physical computer within the physical memory of the host machine, but completely separated from the underlying hardware of the host machine

Introduction to VMware ESXi on Linux

VMware allows multiple operating systems and applications to run independently in virtual machines, as shown in Figure 2-1. A *virtual machine* is a software implementation of a computer that executes programs as if it were a real physical computer within the physical memory of the host machine, but completely separated from the underlying hardware of the host machine.

This can be extremely useful for disaster recovery, because it takes less time to get a new virtual machine up and running should it fail than it takes to get a new physical server up and running. This chapter teaches you how to use several VMware software solutions, including ESX/ESXi, vSphere, and vCenter.

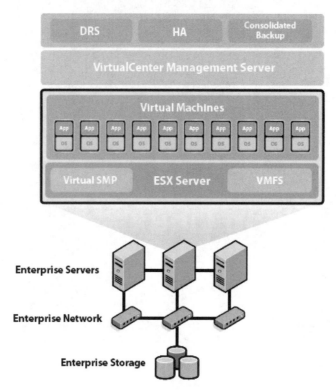

Figure 2-1   With VMware, multiple virtual machines can be run at once.

VMware and Business Continuity

Figures 2-2 through 2-7 show the following advantages of using VMware for business continuity:

- High availability without complex configurations
- Cost-effective failover clustering
- Continuity with virtual machines on storage area networks (SAN)
- Storage array–based replication
- Virtualized failover site
- Backup operations

VMware and Disaster Recovery

VMware has the following uses for disaster recovery:

- Partitioning
  - Allows for the consolidation of several applications and operating systems on the same machine, increasing server utilization
  - Provides considerable operational savings
- Hardware independence
  - Hastens recovery by simplifying system startup and configuration at the disaster recovery site
  - Minimizes the cost of buying similar, new recovery servers

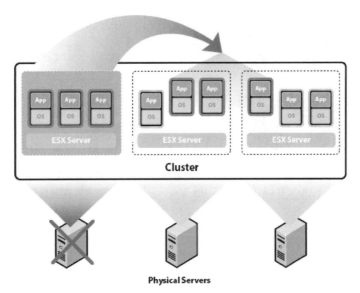

Figure 2-2 VMware detects server failures, and if one fails, it automatically restarts virtual machines on different physical servers.

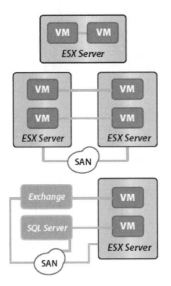

Figure 2-3 VMware uses clustering to distribute workloads across several machines, yielding availability benefits.

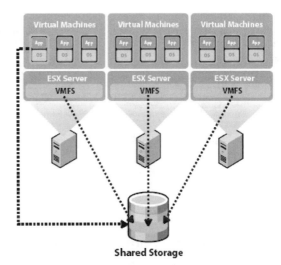

Figure 2-4 Storage area networks allow data to survive server failures.

- Encapsulation
  - Stores server operating system, applications, data, configurations, and state as an image file on the hard disk
  - Simplifies operations including backup and recovery, server migration, duplication, and disaster recovery server provisioning

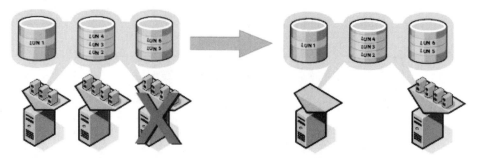

Figure 2-5 Storage array–based replication creates exact copies of data and applications at remote locations so they are ready to activate when necessary.

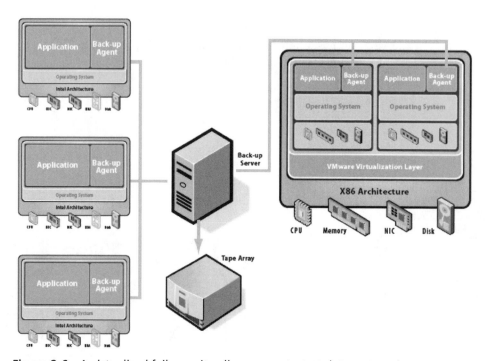

Figure 2-6 A virtualized failover site allows users to test data restoration.

- Isolation
  - Changes in any virtual machine are entirely isolated from other virtual machines
  - A user can simultaneously run batch programs and disaster recovery tests on the disaster recovery hardware

The encapsulation process is shown in Figure 2-8, while the isolation process is shown in Figure 2-9.

VMware ESX

VMware ESX partitions servers into virtual machines, reducing hardware and power requirements. Its features include the following:

- Single-server partitioning
- Production-class hypervisor

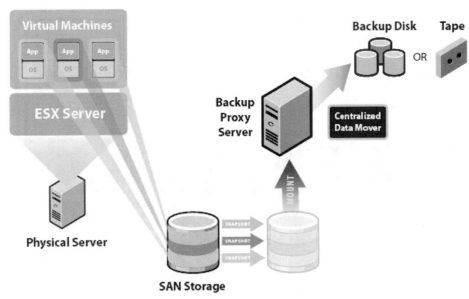

Figure 2-7 The VMware backup agent reliably controls the backup and file restoration process.

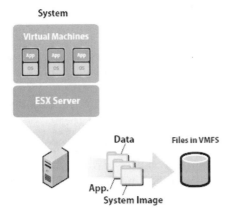

Figure 2-8 VMware can store a system's hard drive image in a single file for easy recovery.

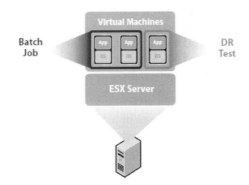

Figure 2-9 VMware isolates changes on one virtual machine from others.

- Advanced server resource management
- Shared physical resources
- Runs unmodified operating systems and applications
- Runs demanding applications side by side on the same server

ESX is platform independent, requires minimal interfaces, and can run multiple operating systems on a single server. It has a protected, menu-driven interface to prevent users from running arbitrary code. Users do not need experience with any particular OS, and no user accounts or passwords are required to be created and maintained. No operating system antivirus software or backup efforts are required.

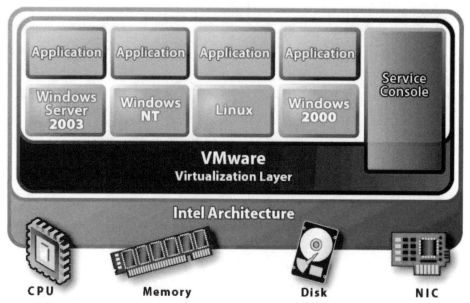

Figure 2-10 VMware ESX Server allocates hardware resources to multiple workloads.

VMware ESX supports both Windows and Linux. It replaces the scripting execution environment of the service console, using the same commands and same syntax as VMware Infrastructure 3. It provides standards-based monitoring of hardware resources.

VMware ESX Server System Architecture

VMware ESX Server provides resource management services, as well as a service console providing bootstrapping, management, and other services. The ESX Server architecture allocates available hardware resources to multiple workloads on a remote network.

VMware ESX Server's architecture is shown in Figure 2-10. Key elements of the system's design include the following:

- The virtualization layer virtualizes the hardware environment and physical resources so that they are accessible to multiple users without any interference.

- The resource manager is used for enabling partitions as well as allocating memory, CPU time, disk use, and network bandwidth to all virtual machines.

- The hardware interface components include device drivers and are used to enable hardware-specific service delivery. While enabling hardware-specific service delivery, these components hide hardware differences from other parts of the system.

- VMware ESX allows the user to run multiple applications in virtual machines on the same physical server.

Installing ESX Server 3i on Linux

To install ESX Server 3i on a Linux system, a user follows these steps:

1. Plug the network cable into the Ethernet adapter.

2. Insert the VMware ESX Server CD and boot the machine.

3. If required, set the CD-ROM as the first boot device at the BIOS setup screen.

4. At the boot prompt, type **text** and press Enter.

5. At the **Welcome** screen, read the acknowledgment message and click **OK** to continue.

6. The installer will scan the system hardware to determine if the Ethernet and SCSI devices are compatible with VMware ESX Server.

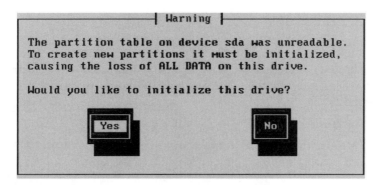

Figure 2-11   Click **Yes** to format the device.

7. At the **Installation Type** screen, select a suitable installation type from the following, and then click **OK**:

   • *Default*: Performs a full installation and clears any existing data on the selected partitions.

   • *Custom*: Allows the user to manually select keyboard and mouse configuration options.

   • *Upgrade Existing System*: Upgrades an existing installation of the ESX Server.

8. If **Custom** is selected, set the keyboard and mouse options, then click **OK** after each.

9. The **End User License Agreement** screen should appear. Check **Accept End User License**, then click **OK**.

10. Enter the ESX Server serial number in the **ESX Serial Number** field, then click **OK**.

11. If installing ESX Server on an unformatted disk, the warning message in Figure 2-11 will appear. Click **Yes** to continue.

12. The **Disk Partitioning Setup** screen will then appear. The ESX Server system requires a minimum of three partitions. Select **Manual** to manually create the partitions, or select **Automatic** to have the installer create the partitions. If the **Automatic** option is selected, then specify the hard disk space to be allocated to the service console by selecting the appropriate option, and click **OK**. If **Manual** is selected, follow these steps:

   • To create the first partition, click **New**. Set the mount point to /boot, the type to ext3, and the size to 50 MB.

   • To create the second partition, click **New**. Set no mount point, the type to swap, and the size to double the memory assigned to the service console.

   • To create the third partition, click **New**. Set the mount point to /, the type to ext3, and the size to 1800 MB.

13. At the **Network Configuration** screen, enter the following information and select **OK** to continue:

   • Enter the host's name in the **Hostname** entry field.

   • Check the **Use bootp/dhcp** box.

   • In the **IP address** block, enter the IP address, subnet mask, and network gateway.

   • Enter the primary and secondary domain name servers.

14. The **Time Zone Selection** screen appears. Select the local time zone and then click **OK**.

15. On the **Root Password** screen, specify the new root password and click **OK**. Note that *root* is the username for the administrator. Users with administrative privileges log in with this name when using the VMware Management Interface or the service console.

16. At the **Add User** screen, add at least one user and then click **OK**.

17. At the **User Account Setup** screen, user accounts can be added, edited, or deleted. Click **OK** to move on.

18. The **Installation to Begin** screen appears. Click **OK** to begin installing files.

19. Once the packages are installed, the **Complete** screen appears. Click **OK** to reboot and finish the installation.

Configuring ESX Server 3i

To configure an installed ESX Server system, a user follows these steps:

1. Launch a Web browser and enter the URL as **http://** followed by the hostname assigned to the server during the ESX Server installation. For example, if the hostname is 192.168.1.5, enter the URL as **http://192.168.1.5**.

2. Accept the site's security certificate.

3. Log in to the VMware Management Interface as *root* using the credentials entered during installation.

4. The System Configuration Wizard will launch. Click the **Next** button to start the wizard.

5. The **End User License Agreement** appears. Check the **I accept the terms of the license agreement** check box, and enter the VMware ESX Server serial number in the **VMware ESX Server** field. Click the **Next** button.

6. At the **Startup Profile** screen, configure the following parameters, and then click the **Next** button:

   - *Reserved memory*: The default reserved memory for the service console is 192 MB, which is enough for managing up to eight virtual machines concurrently. To manage more than eight virtual machines, use the following values:

     - 272 MB for up to 16 virtual machines.
     - 384 MB for up to 32 virtual machines.
     - 512 MB for more than 32 virtual machines.

   - *SCSI Storage Controller*: Select the storage adapters to be used by the service console and virtual machines on the server. To use the same adapter for both the service console and virtual machines, in the **Dedicated To** list, select **Virtual Machines**, and then check **Shared with Service Console**.

   - *Ethernet Controllers*: Select the network adapters to be used by the service console and virtual machines on the server.

   - Check the **Enable Hyper-threading** check box to enable the ESX Server to boot in hyperthreading mode.

7. At the **Reboot** screen, click the **Next** button to reboot the system.

8. After the reboot, log in again.

9. The **Storage Management** screen appears. At this screen, you can do any of the following and then click the **Next** button to continue:

   - Create new VMFS-2 partitions to store virtual machines in any remaining free space.
   - Edit the existing VMFS volumes.
   - Remove any extended partitions.

10. At the **Swap Configuration** screen, set up the swap file that ESX Server uses as part of its memory management features. The default configuration creates a swap file equal to the total amount of memory on the server.

    - Click **Change** to make any required changes to the swap file configuration.
    - If there is a configured swap file, click **Activate** or **Edit** to activate or edit the configured swap file.
    - If there is no configured swap file, click **Create** to create and configure a swap file.
    - Click **Next** to continue.

11. Set the following swap file settings, and click the **Next** button to continue:

    - VMFS volume.
    - File name.
    - File size.
    - Activation policy.

12. The **Network Connections** screen appears, showing the system's virtual switches.

    - Click **Add** to create a new virtual switch.
    - For an existing virtual switch, click **Add** to create a port group and assign a label and VLAN ID for the new port group.

- Click **Edit** to configure the speed and duplex settings for the virtual switch.
- Click the **Next** button to continue.

13. At the **Security Settings** screen, select the security level for the ESX Server machine and the network traffic generated by the ESX Server. To use custom settings, check the **Custom Security** check box and click the **Next** button.

14. At the **Custom Security Configuration** screen, customize the security settings by choosing the proper options and click the **OK** button.

15. After choosing security settings, click the **Next** button. A message appears stating that configuration is complete. Click the **OK** button to finish configuration.

VMware vSphere

VMware vSphere uses virtualization to convert data centers into simplified cloud-computing infrastructures. Cloud computing is a general term used to describe the providing of computing services via a network connection such as the Internet. Physical hardware resources across multiple systems are virtualized and become a group, offering virtual resources to the data center. vSphere manages large pools of infrastructure such as networking, CPUs, and storage as a flawless dynamic operating environment.

The VMware vSphere client can be downloaded from the VMware server's Web interface. Figure 2-12 is a diagram of VMware vSphere.

VMware vSphere Component Layers

The following are the component layers of VMware vSphere:

- *Infrastructure services*: These services are provided to abstract, collect, and allot infrastructure resources and hardware. These services include:

  - *VMware vCompute*: Abstracts away from underlying discrete server resources and collects and assigns these resources across distinct servers to applications

  - *VMware vStorage*: Allows for the efficient use and management of storage

  - *VMware vNetwork*: Simplifies and enhances networking

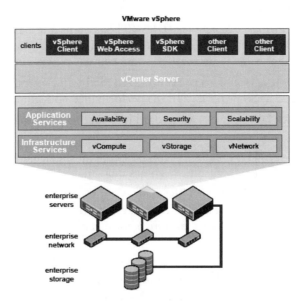

Figure 2-12 VMware vSphere virtualizes physical resources together.

- *Application services*: These ensure scalability, availability, and security. Some examples include fault tolerance and high-availability (HA) applications.
- *VMware vCenter Server*: This offers a single control point for the data center and provides services such as configuration, performance monitoring, and access control.
- *Clients*: Users access the VMware vSphere data center through clients like the vSphere client and Web access through a Web browser.

VMware vSphere Components

The following are the components of VMware vSphere:

- *VMware ESX and ESXi*: The virtualization layer runs on physical servers that abstract storage, processor, memory, and other resources into multiple virtual machines. ESX can be embedded into a server's firmware, or it can be separately installed software. There are two versions of ESX:
  - VMware ESX 4.0 contains a built-in server console that is available as an installable CD-ROM boot image.
  - VMware ESXi 4.0 does not contain a server console and is provided as either embedded or installed.
- *VMware vCenter Server*: This is the central point for provisioning, configuring, and managing virtualized IT environments.
- *VMware vSphere Client*: This interface allows users to remotely connect to ESX/ESXi or vCenter Server from any Windows PC.
- *VMware vSphere Web Access*: This Web interface allows access to remote consoles and virtual management.
- *VMware Virtual Machine File System (VMFS)*: This is a high-performance cluster file system for ESX/ESXi virtual machines.
- *VMware Virtual SMP*: This allows a single virtual machine to concurrently use multiple physical processors.
- *VMware VMotion*: This allows for the live migration of running virtual machines from one physical server to another with continuous service availability, zero downtime, and complete transaction integrity.
- *Storage VMotion*: This enables the migration of virtual machine files from one database to another without service interruption.
- *VMware High Availability (HA)*: This offers high availability for applications running in virtual machines. Failing servers are restarted on other production servers that have sufficient capacity.
- *VMware Distributed Resource Scheduler (DRS)*: This assigns and balances computing capacity dynamically across the pool of hardware resources for virtual machines. It includes Distributed Power Management (DPM) that helps to decrease the data center's power consumption.
- *VMware Consolidated Backup*: This is a centralized facility for agent-free backup of virtual machines. It reduces the impact of backups on ESX/ESXi performance and simplifies backup administration.
- *VMware vSphere SDK*: This provides a standard interface for third party and VMware solutions for accessing the VMware vSphere.
- *VMware Fault Tolerance*: This creates a secondary copy of the original virtual machine, which becomes active when the primary virtual machine becomes unavailable, providing continuous availability.
- *vNetwork Distributed Switch (DVS)*: This involves a distributed virtual machine that spans the ESX/ESXi hosts, allowing for increased network capacity and the reduction of ongoing network maintenance activities. This way, virtual machines maintain a consistent network configuration as they migrate across multiple hosts.
- *Host profiles*: This simplifies host configuration management through user-defined policies. Host profile policies check compliance to standard host configuration settings across the data center.
- *Pluggable storage architecture*: This is a multipath I/O framework that allows storage partners to enable their array asynchronously to ESX release schedules.

Physical Topology of a vSphere Data Center

A VMware vSphere data center includes the following physical components:

- *Computing servers*: These are industry-standard x86 servers that run ESX/ESXi on bare metal. Computing servers are called **standalone hosts** in a virtualized environment. To provide a pool of resources in the virtual environment, similarly configured x86 servers can be grouped with connections to the same storage subsystems and network.

- *Storage networks and arrays*: Storage technologies such as iSCSI SAN arrays, Fibre Channel SAN arrays, and NAS arrays are used to meet data center storage needs. Storage arrays are shared among groups of servers using storage area networks. This results in a pool of storage resources.

- *IP networks*: Multiple Ethernet network interface cards (NICs) provide reliable networking and high bandwidth to the VMware vSphere data center.

- *vCenter Server*: This provides a single point of control to the data center, with services such as performance monitoring, configuration, and access control. Resources from individual hosts are connected by vCenter Server, which shares them among virtual machines. This is done by managing the assignment of resources to the virtual machine and the assignment of virtual machines to computing servers. vCenter Server allows for the utilization of advanced vSphere features such as VMware VMotion, VMware Distributed Resource Scheduler (DRS), and VMware High Availability (HA).

- *Management clients*: Many interfaces such as VMware vSphere Client, vSphere Command-Line Interface, Web access, and vSphere Management Assistant are provided by VMware vSphere for virtual machine access and data center management.

Figure 2-13 shows the physical topology of a vSphere data center.

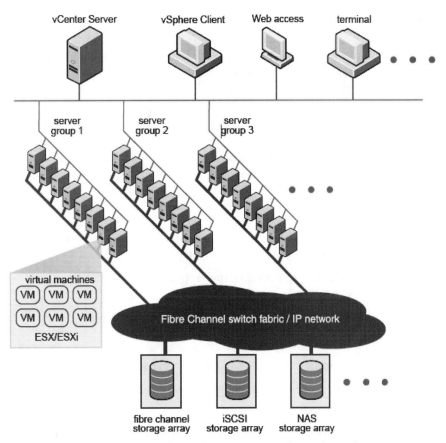

Figure 2-13   These are the physical components of a vSphere data center.

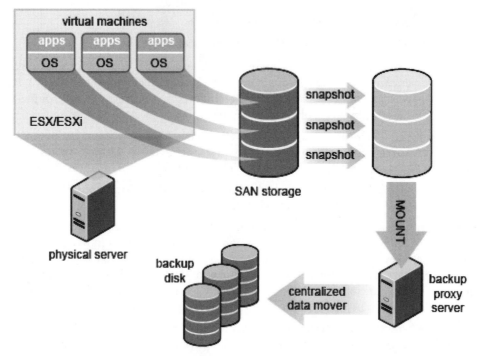

Figure 2-14   VMware Consolidated Backup backs up data to a separate server.

VMware Consolidated Backup

The VMware vSphere storage architecture enables VMware Consolidated Backup, which provides a centralized facility for LAN-free backup of virtual machines. Consolidated Backup works in conjunction with a third-party backup agent residing on a separate backup proxy server (not on the server running ESX/ESXi). It does not require an agent inside the virtual machines, so it provides a simple backup solution with low overhead.

VMware Consolidated Backup is shown in Figure 2-14.

Adding a Virtual Machine by Importing a Virtual Appliance

A virtual machine can be added to a host after connecting to the host machine. One or more virtual machines can be imported or created on a single host. A new virtual machine can be built manually, or a virtual appliance can be imported from the VMware Web site. A virtual appliance is a prebuilt virtual machine with an operating system and applications already installed. The vSphere Client's **Getting Started** tab, shown in Figure 2-15, facilitates both options.

VMware recommends importing a virtual appliance as the first virtual machine. To add a virtual machine by importing a virtual appliance, users can follow these steps:

1. In the **Getting Started** tab, click **Import a virtual appliance**.

2. Choose **VA Marketplace** and then click **Next**.

3. Choose a virtual appliance from the list and click **Download now**.

4. Click **Next** and follow the on-screen instructions.

After the virtual appliance is imported, users can follow these steps:

1. Use the **Console** tab in the vSphere Client to power on the virtual appliance and view it.

2. Press Ctrl+Alt to release the pointer from its control.

3. From the inventory, right-click the virtual machine and select **Open Console** to view the console in full-screen mode.

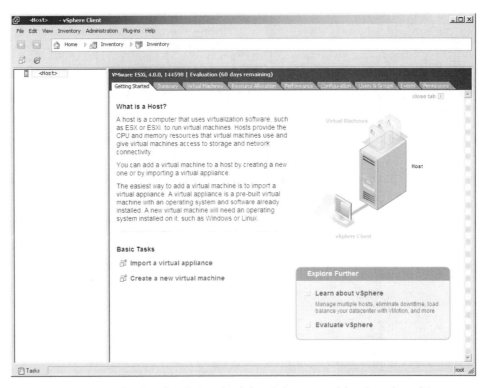

Figure 2-15   Go to the **Getting Started** tab in vSphere to add a virtual machine.

VMware vCenter Server

VMware vCenter Server provides centralized management for data centers. It aggregates physical resources from multiple ESX/ESXi hosts and presents a central collection of simple and flexible resources for the system administrator. The following are the components of VMware vCenter Server, shown in Figure 2-16:

- *User access control*: This enables the administrator to create and manage different levels of access for different users.
- *Core services*: These are the basic management services for the virtual data center, including:
  - Virtual machine provisioning
  - Host and virtual machine configuration
  - Resource and virtual machine inventory management
  - Alarms and events management
  - Task scheduler
  - Consolidation
  - vApp
- *Distributed services*: These extend vSphere capabilities beyond a single physical server. Some of these services include VMware VMotion, VMware DRS, and VMware HA. Distributed services allow these solutions to be configured and managed from vCenter Server.
- *Plug-ins*: These are applications that add additional functionality and features. They can be installed on top of vCenter Server. Plug-ins include:
  - VMware vCenter Converter
  - VMware Update Manager

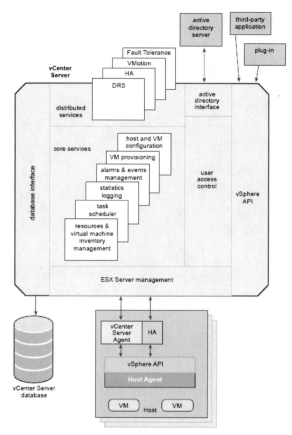

Figure 2-16 These are the components of VMware vCenter Server.

- *vCenter Server interfaces*: These integrate vCenter Server with third-party applications and products. There are four key interfaces:
  - *ESX management*: Manages each physical server in the data center by interfacing with the vCenter Server agent
  - *VMware vSphere API*: Interfaces with third-party clients and VMware management clients
  - *Database interface*: Stores information such as host configurations, virtual machine configurations, resource and virtual machine inventory, events, alarms, performance statistics, user permissions, and roles by connecting to Microsoft SQL Server, Oracle, or IBM DB2
  - *Active Directory interface*: Obtains user access control information by connecting to Active Directory

vCenter Server Installation

Before installing vCenter Server, administrators must make sure the following prerequisites are met:

- Obtain an installation DVD or download the installation ISO image.
- Ensure that the hardware meets the hardware requirements of the vCenter Server.
- Upgrade the existing Virtual Center installed on the machine.
- Ensure that Network Address Translation (NAT) is open between the vCenter Server system and the hosts it manages.
- It may be beneficial to install the bundled SQL Server 2005 Express database on one of the operating systems.
- Ensure that the connection between the domain controller and machine is working during the installation.
- The computer name should not be longer than 15 characters.

- The actual computer name and the DNS name should be matched.
- Ensure that the system is not an Active Directory domain controller.
- The domain user account of systems running vCenter Server should have the following permissions:
  - Log on as a service
  - Act as part of the operating system
  - Member of the administrators group
- A Windows server hosting the vCenter Server system should be assigned a static IP address and hostname.
- If Windows Server 2003 SP1 is installed with vCenter Server, the disk for the installation directory must be in NTFS format.
- The system must belong to a domain rather than a workgroup.

To install vCenter Server, a user follows these steps:

1. Open the installation program.
2. Click **vCenter Server**.
3. Select the language for the installer and click **OK**.
4. Click the **Next** button on the **Welcome** screen.
5. Check the **I agree to the terms in the license agreement** check box, and click the **Next** button.
6. Enter the username, organization name, and vCenter Server license key, and click the **Next** button.
7. Choose the database type to be used:
   - If using the bundled database, click **Install a Microsoft SQL Server 2005 Express instance**.
   - If using an existing database, click **Use an existing supported database** and choose the database from the list of DSNs (database source names). Click the **Next** button after typing the username and password for the DSN.
8. Provide the administrator name and password to be used, and click the **Next** button.
9. Check the **Use SYSTEM Account** check box and click the **Next** button.
10. Accept the default destination folders and click the **Next** button.
11. Click the **Create a standalone VMware vCenter Server instance or join group** button and click the **Next** button.
12. If in a group, enter the domain name and LDAP port number of any remote vCenter Server system and click the **Next** button.
13. Accept the default port numbers for all the components, or enter custom port numbers, and click the **Next** button.
14. Click the **Install** button.
15. Click the **Finish** button.

Security for ESX Server 3i Systems

All VMware virtual machines are isolated from one another, which is unnoticeable to the guest operating system. Even a user with an administrative or kernel system-level access on a guest operating system cannot break the isolation layer to access another virtual machine without rights openly granted by the ESX Server system administrator.

Isolation of the multiple virtual machines provides security during hardware sharing and ensures uninterrupted performance and the virtual machines' ability to access hardware. A guest operating system crash has no effect on:

- The ability of users to access other virtual machines
- The ability of operational virtual machines to access the resources they need
- The performance of other virtual machines

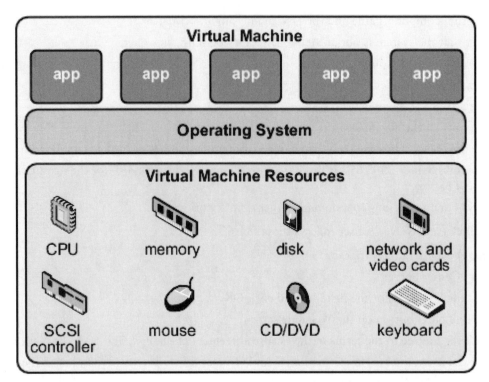

Figure 2-17 Every virtual machine is isolated from other virtual machines running on the same hardware.

Virtual machines share physical resources such as CPU, memory, and I/O devices, but the guest OS cannot detect any device other than the virtual devices made available to it. All access to physical resources takes place through the VMkernel. With the help of the virtual switch, virtual machines can communicate with other virtual machines running on the same ESX Server host. They can also communicate with the physical network with the help of a physical network adapter.

Figure 2-17 shows the isolation of virtual machines.

Recommendations for Securing VMware ESX

The following are some recommendations for securing ESX:

- Always use firewall and antivirus software for the console operating system (COS).
- Use VLANs to segment the physical network.
- When installing ESX, use the highest security level.
- Do not allow root level access over SSH, and use secure commands.
- Disable or stop all unnecessary services in the COS.
- Keep ESX patched to the most current version.
- Secure guest operating systems.
- Use vCenter Server to control user-level access.
- Document and monitor configuration changes.

Chapter Summary

- VMware ESX partitions servers into virtual machines, reducing hardware and power requirements.
- VMware ESX Server provides resource management services and a service console that provides boot-strapping, management, and other services.

- The ESX Server architecture is responsible for allocating available hardware resources to multiple workloads on a remote network.
- The VMware virtualization layer virtualizes the hardware environment and physical resources so that they are accessible to multiple users without any interference.

Review Questions

1. What is the VMware infrastructure?

   _____
   _____
   _____
   _____

2. How can VMware save an organization money and time?

   _____
   _____
   _____
   _____

3. What is VMware ESX?

   _____
   _____
   _____
   _____

4. What is the VMware ESX Server architecture?

   _____
   _____
   _____
   _____

5. What are the key elements of VMware ESX Server's design?

   _____
   _____
   _____
   _____

6. What is virtual machine isolation?

   _____
   _____
   _____
   _____

7. How does virtual machine isolation provide security?

   _____
   _____
   _____
   _____

Hands-On Projects

1. Install VMware ESX Server 3.

   ▪ Navigate to Chapter 2 of the Student Resource Center and click on the link to download VMWare ESX Server 4.

   ▪ Launch the ESX Server 4 installer.

   ▪ Press Enter to install VMware ESXi.

   ▪ Press F11 to accept the terms and conditions.

   ▪ Press Enter to select a disk and continue.

   ▪ Press F11 to confirm the installation.

   ▪ Press Enter to reboot the system.

   ▪ Click **Configure Password** to set a new password.

   ▪ Provide a new password to prevent unauthorized access to the host machine and press the **OK** button.

   ▪ Disable **Configure Lockdown Mode** and press Enter so that remote users are not prevented from logging into the host machine using the root logon name.

   ▪ Click **Configure Management Network** and press Enter to view and modify the host's management network settings.

   ▪ Click **Restart Management Network** and press Enter to restore networking.

   ▪ Click Test **Management Network** and press Enter to perform a brief network test.

   ▪ Click **Disable Management Network** and press Enter to disable the management network.

   ▪ Click **Configure Keyboard** and press Enter to select the layout type for the keyboard of the host machine.

   ▪ Click **View Support Information** to view the serial number, license serial number, and SSL thumbprint.

   ▪ Click **View System Logs** and press Esc to view messages, configuration information, and the Management Agent.

   ▪ Click **Restart Management Agents** and press Enter to disconnect all remote management software.

   ▪ Click **Reset System Configuration** and press Enter to revert the software to its default settings.

   ▪ Click **Remove Custom Extensions** and press Enter to remove all custom extensions.

   ▪ Press F12 to shut down or restart the host machine.

   ▪ Open a Web browser and type **http://** followed by the internal IP of the server machine as the URL and press Enter.

   ▪ Download the vSphere Client installer from the **VMware ESXi Welcome** page.

   ▪ Install the vSphere Client.

   ▪ Provide the IP address/hostname, username, and password to log into the vSphere Client.

   ▪ Click **System Logs** to view the log entries.

   ▪ Click **Inventory** and then **Create a new virtual machine**.

   ▪ Select the configuration type for the virtual machine and click **Next**.

   ▪ Select the guest operating system for the virtual machine and click **Next**.

   ▪ Specify the virtual disk space and provisioning policy for the virtual machine and click **Next**.

- Click **Finish** to create the new virtual machine.
- Explore what you can do with this new virtual machine from the vSphere Client.

2. Read about ESX3 best practices.
   - Navigate to Chapter 2 of the Student Resource Center.
   - Open esx3_best_practices.pdf and read the content.

3. Read about ESX Server 3i architecture.
   - Navigate to Chapter 2 of the Student Resource Center.
   - Open ESXServer3i_architecture.pdf and read the content.

4. Read about Site Recovery Manager.
   - Navigate to Chapter 2 of the Student Resource Center.
   - Open srm_10_api.pdf and read the content.

## Chapter 3

Microsoft Virtualization

Objectives

After completing this chapter, you should be able to:

- Discuss Microsoft virtualization
- Give an overview of virtualization with Hyper-V
- Install Hyper-V
- Install a virtual machine
- Create Hyper-V Server virtual networks
- Configure virtual networks
- Add a network adapter to a VM

Key Terms

Hypervisor   a thin layer of software that can run multiple operating systems on a single server simultaneously

Role-based access control   an access control strategy that enables the user to specify access control in terms of the organizational structure of a company

Virtualization stack   a group of software components that cooperate to support virtual machines

Introduction to Microsoft Virtualization

Virtualization is a framework or methodology that divides the resources of a computer into multiple execution environments. Microsoft virtualization solutions work in the same way as Windows-based interfaces and technologies. Microsoft virtualization technologies can be used to manage physical and virtual IT resources across multiple operating systems and hypervisors, from the data center to the desktop. In Microsoft virtualization, the centralized management system combines all the virtualization products and technologies together, as shown in Figure 3-1.

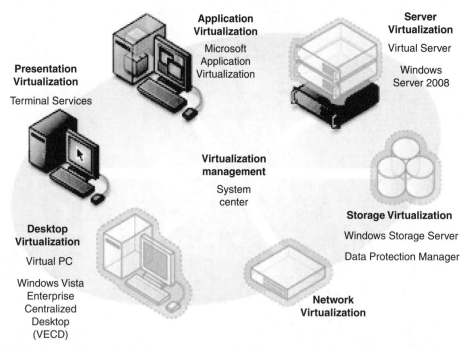

Figure 3-1 The centralized management system combines Microsoft virtualization products and technologies.

Virtualization with Hyper-V

Windows Server 2008 Hyper-V is a server-based virtualization technology that consolidates multiple server roles. Using Hyper-V, different operating systems, such as Linux, can be operated along with Windows on a single server. Administrators can use Hyper-V's Authorization Manager and provide role-based access control to resources. Administrators using Hyper-V can also minimize the errors that occur because of misconfigured resources. Microsoft Hyper-V is a 64-bit virtualization technology that accomplishes the following goals:

- Reduced costs
- Increased hardware utilization
- Optimized network and business infrastructure
- Improved server availability

Key Features of Hyper-V

- *64-bit architecture*: 64-bit microkernelized hypervisor architecture enables Hyper-V to provide a broad array of device support methods and improved performance and security.

- *Broad OS support*: Hyper-V supports simultaneously running different types of operating systems, including 32-bit and 64-bit systems, across different server platforms, such as Windows, Linux, and others.

- *Symmetric Multiprocessors (SMP) support*: Ability to support up to four multiple processors in a virtual machine environment enables the user to take full advantage of the multithreaded applications in a virtual machine.

- *Network load balancing*: Hyper-V includes virtual-switch capabilities. This means virtual machines can be configured to run with the Windows Network Load Balancing (NLB) service to balance the load across virtual machines on different servers.

- *Hardware-sharing architecture*: With virtual service provider/virtual service client (VSP/VSC) architecture, Hyper-V provides improved access and utilization of core resources, such as disk, networking, and video.

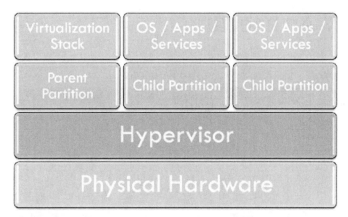

Figure 3-2   A hypervisor can run multiple operating systems on a single server by using multiple layers.

- *Quick migration*: Hyper-V enables the user to rapidly migrate a running virtual machine from one physical host system to another with minimal downtime, leveraging familiar high-availability capabilities of the Windows Server and System Center management tools.

- *Virtual machine snapshot*: Hyper-V can take snapshots of a running virtual machine so the user can revert to a previous state, improving overall backup and recoverability capabilities.

- *Scalability*: With support for multiple processors and cores at the host level and improved memory access within virtual machines, the user can vertically scale the virtualization environment to support a large number of virtual machines within a given host and continue to leverage quick migration for scalability across multiple hosts.

- *Extensibility*: Standards-based Windows Management Instrumentation (WMI) interfaces and APIs in Hyper-V enable independent software vendors and developers to quickly build custom tools, utilities, and enhancements for the virtualization platform.

Hyper-V Technology

A *hypervisor* (Figure 3-2) is a thin layer of software that can run multiple operating systems on a single server simultaneously. This technology makes it easier to interact with hardware, operating systems, and virtual machines simultaneously and makes the core virtualization components stronger. The hypervisor software runs directly on the hardware platform. It also runs under all the operating systems running on the computer. The kernel communicates with the hypervisor to provide the best performance and scalability. The hypervisor performs like a kernel in the following ways:

- Manages memory
- Schedules threads
- Handles basic functionality of the system

Hyper-V Architecture

Hyper-V supports isolation using partitions in which the operating system is running, as shown in Figure 3-3. It uses a parent partition that runs either a full installation of Windows Server 2008 or a Server Core installation. The parent partition provides an environment with small space to run specific server roles. The *virtualization stack* is a group of software components that cooperate to support the virtual machines. It cannot access hardware resources directly. The virtualization stack requests are delivered through the parent partition via a virtual machine bus, and the subsystem exchanges requests and data. Shell commands can be used to configure the actual OS, physical hardware, and software.

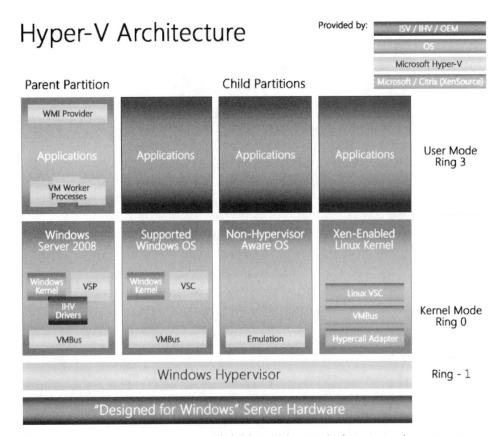

Figure 3-3   Hyper-V uses parent and child partitions to isolate operating systems.

Hyper-V in Business Continuity and Disaster Recovery

Disaster recovery is a key component and plays an important role during business continuity processes. Business continuity helps to minimize both scheduled and unscheduled downtime in case of disaster. Hyper-V's business continuity features, such as live backup and quick migration, enable businesses to meet their goals during stringent uptime. Hyper-V helps businesses in disaster recovery and business continuity by restoring the backed-up data during disasters. Disasters can be of any type, including natural disasters, malicious attacks, and configuration problems such as software conflicts. Hyper-V uses its dispersed clustering capabilities to provide solutions during disaster recovery within IT environments and across data centers. Hyper-V's disaster recovery and business continuity solutions ensure minimal data loss.

Security Assumptions Before Designing a Hyper-V Installation

The following security assumptions should be made before designing a Hyper-V installation:

- All the guest users are untrusted.
- The parent is trusted by the hypervisor and the parent is trusted by all the children.
- Code in guests can run in all modes, rings, and segments.
- The hypercall interface should be documented.
- Guests should attempt all hypercalls.
- Make sure the guests are running on a hypervisor.
- The design of the Hyper-V installation should be well understood.

Security Goals for Hyper-V

The following security goals for Hyper-V should be followed in a virtual environment:

- Strong isolation between partitions
- Guest confidentiality and integrity
- Separation of virtual devices
- Separation of VMBus per VM from the parent
- No memory sharing
- No guest-to-guest VM interface communications
- No guest DMA attacks

Installation and Configurations

Installing Hyper-V

The following steps will install Hyper-V:

1. Go to the **Start** menu and click **Server Manager,** as shown in Figure 3-4.
2. Click **Roles** in the **Server Manager** Window, as shown in Figure 3-5.
3. View the health of the roles installed and click **Add Roles,** as shown in Figure 3-6.
4. Click **Next** on the **Add Roles Wizard** page, as shown in Figure 3-7.

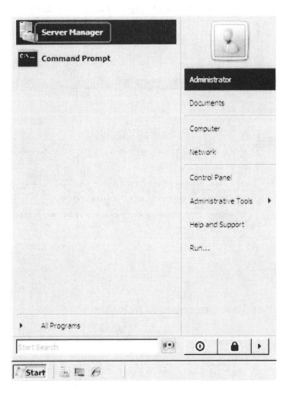

Figure 3-4 Go to the Start menu and click **Server Manager.**

Figure 3-5 Click **Roles** in the
Server Manager Window.

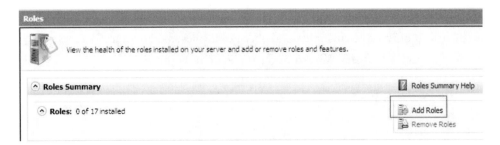

Figure 3-6 View the health of the roles installed and click **Add Roles**.

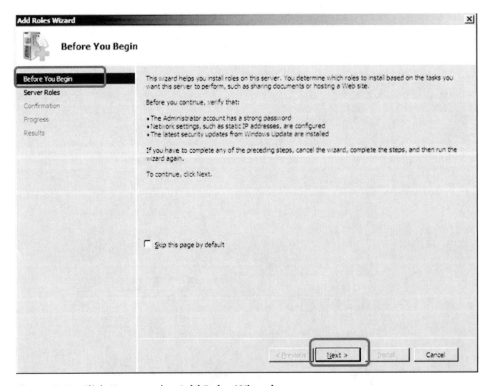

Figure 3-7 Click **Next** on the **Add Roles Wizard** page.

5. Select Hyper-V from the list and click **Next,** as shown in Figure 3-8.

6. Read the introduction to Hyper-V and click **Next,** as shown in Figure 3-9.

7. The **Create Virtual Networks** page will open.

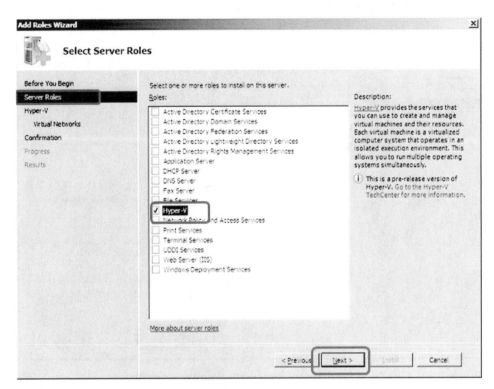

Figure 3-8   Select Hyper-V from the list and click **Next**.

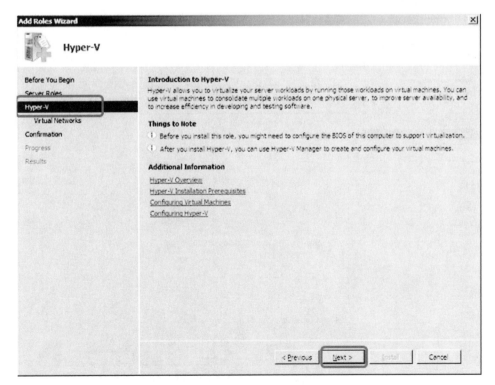

Figure 3-9   Read the introduction to Hyper-V and click **Next**.

8. Click **Next** to create multiple virtual networks on the virtualization server, as shown in Figure 3-10.

9. Go to **Confirmation** in the **Add Roles Wizard** and click **Install,** as shown in Figure 3-11

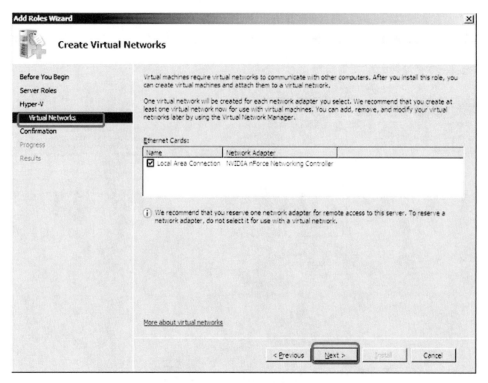

Figure 3-10   Click **Next** to create multiple virtual networks on the
virtualization server.

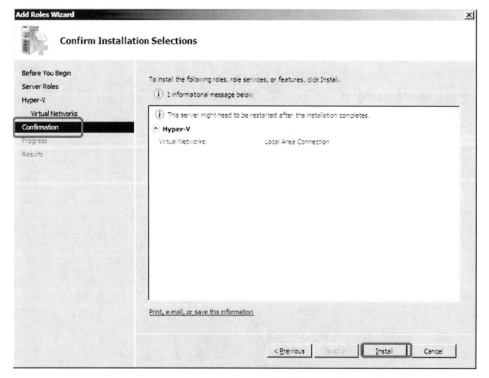

Figure 3-11   Go to **Confirmation** in the **Add Roles Wizard** and click **Install.**

10. View **Installation Progress**, as shown in Figure 3-12.

11. Go to **Results** in the **Add Roles Wizard** and click **Close**, as shown in Figure 3-13.

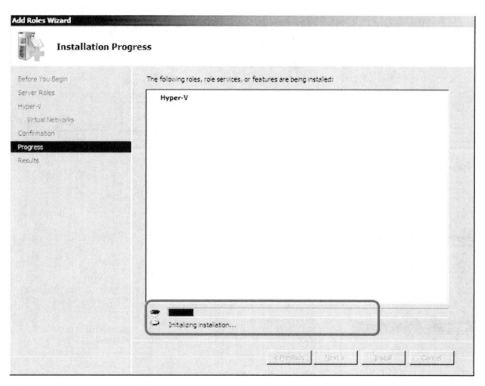

Figure 3-12   View **Installation Progress**.

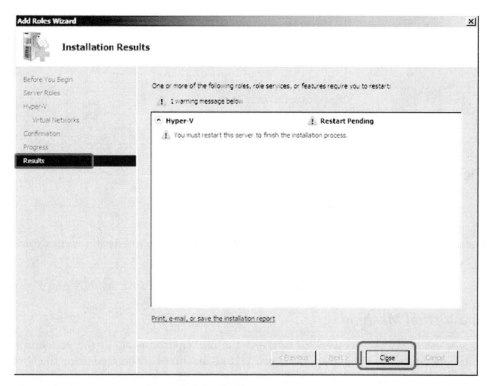

Figure 3-13   Go to **Results** and click **Close**.

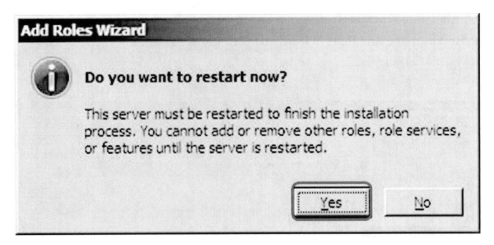

Figure 3-14 Click **Yes** to restart the server.

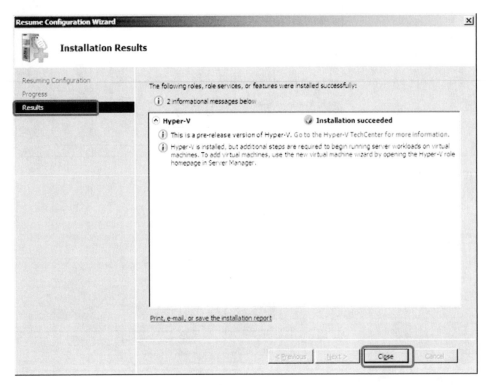

Figure 3-15 Go to **Results** and click **Close**.

12. In the **Add Roles Wizard** dialog box, click **Yes** to restart the server, as shown in Figure 3-14.

13. View progress for resuming the configuration.

14. Go to **Results** in the **Resume Configuration Wizard** and click **Close**, as shown in Figure 3-15.

Creating a Virtual Machine

Hyper-V can be used to run server workloads in a virtualized environment. Virtual machines are created to run different guest operating systems and applications. Virtual machines are created using the New Virtual Machine Wizard. Once a virtual machine is created the user can add, modify, or remove an item by editing the virtual machine's settings, as shown in Figure 3-16.

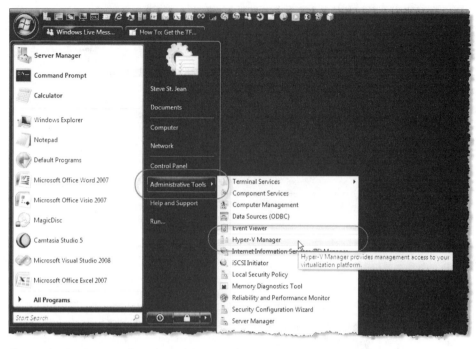

Figure 3-16   Once a virtual machine is created the user can add, modify, or remove an item by editing the virtual machine's settings.

The following steps will configure a virtual machine:

1. Open Hyper-V Manager.

2. Click **Start,** point to **Administrative Tools,** and then click **Hyper-V Manager.**

3. From the **Action** pane, click **New,** and then click **Virtual Machine.**

4. From the **New Virtual Machine Wizard,** click **Next.**

5. On the **Specify Name and Location** page, specify a name for the virtual machine and the location to store it.

6. On the **Memory** page, specify enough memory to run the guest operating system.

7. On the **Networking** page, connect the network adapter to an existing virtual network.

8. On the **Connect Virtual Hard Disk** page, specify a name, location, and size to create a virtual hard disk.

9. On the **Installation Options** page, choose any one of the following:

    • Install an operating system from a boot CD/DVD-ROM

    • Install an operating system from a boot floppy disk

    • Install an operating system from a network-based installation server

10. Click **Finish.**

Configuring a Virtual Machine

1. Click **Start,** point to **Administrative Tools,** and then click **Hyper-V Manager.**

2. In the **Results** pane, under **Virtual Machines,** select a virtual machine.

3. In the Actions pane, under the virtual machine name, click **Hyper-V Settings,** as shown in Figure 3-17.

4. Go to the **Action** tab, click the virtual machine name, and click **Settings.**

5. Go to the **Navigation** tab and click an item to configure.

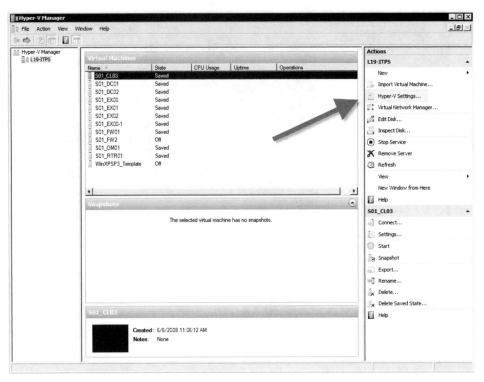

Figure 3-17 In the **Actions** pane, click **Settings**.

6. Add, modify, or remove an item:
   - To add an item, select the item and click **Add.**
   - To modify an item, make changes to the item and click **OK.**
   - To remove an item, select an item and click **Remove.**
7. To make more changes, click the next item to configure, go to Step 6, and continue.
8. Click **OK** once the configuration is completed.

Creating Hyper-V Server Virtual Networks

An administrator uses the following steps to create a Hyper-V Server virtual network:

1. Launch the Hyper-V Manager from a system running Windows Server 2008 or Microsoft Windows Vista SP1 with the Hyper-V Manager management pack loaded.
2. Go to the MMC window and click **Hyper-V Manager.**
3. Go to the **Actions** menu and click **Connect to Server**, select **Another Computer**, and specify the name or IP address of the server to connect to.
4. In the **Actions** menu, click **Virtual Network Manager.**
5. Under **Create virtual network**, select **External** and click **Add**, as shown in Figure 3-18.
6. Enter a name for the new virtual network and click **OK**, as shown in Figure 3-19.

Configuring Virtual Networks

Hyper-V also allows the creation of virtual networks, as shown in Figure 3-20. The following steps will configure a virtual network:

1. Go to the **Start** menu, select **Administrative Tools**, and then click **Hyper-V Manager.**
2. Go to the **Actions** menu and click **Virtual Network Manager.**

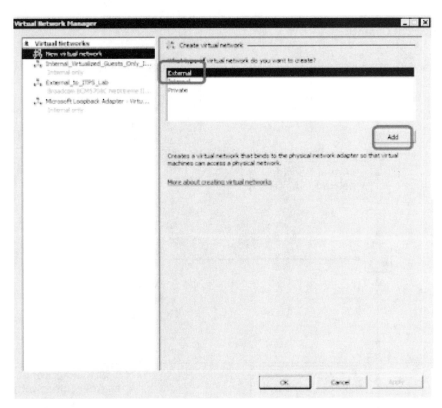

Figure 3-18   Select **External** and click **Add**.

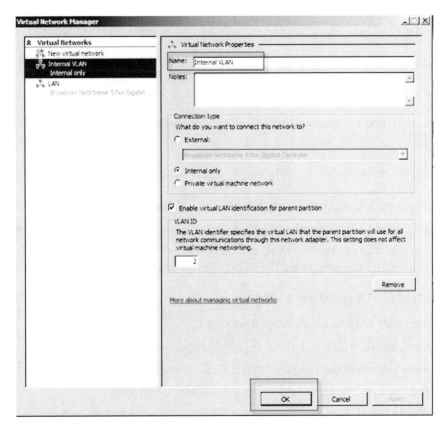

Figure 3-19   Enter a name for the new virtual network and click **OK**.

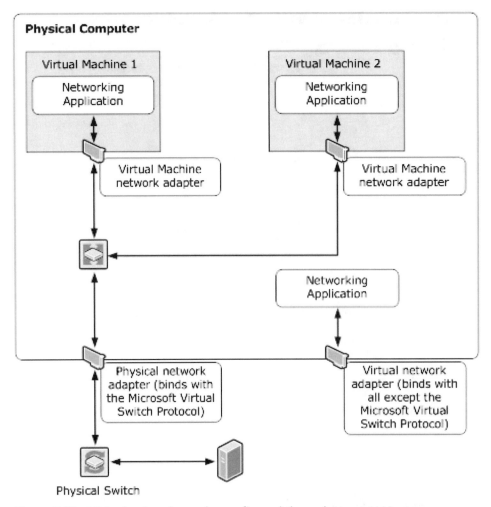

Figure 3-20 Virtual networks can be configured through Hyper-V Manager.

3. Go to **Create virtual network** and select any type from the following:
   - External
   - Internal
   - Private

4. Click **Add**; the **New Virtual Network** page appears.

5. Type a name for the new network, review the other properties, and modify them if necessary.

6. Click **OK** to create the virtual network and close Virtual Network Manager, or click **Apply** to create the virtual network and continue using the Virtual Network Manager.

Adding a Network Adapter to a VM

The following steps will add a network adapter to a VM:

1. Go to **Administrative Tools** and open Hyper-V Manager.

2. Go to **Results** and select the virtual machine under **Virtual Machine**.

3. Go to **Action** and click **Settings** under the virtual machine's name.

4. Go to **Navigation** and click **Add Hardware.**

5. Select a NIC on the **Add Hardware** page.

6. Click **Add**; the **Network Adapter** or **Legacy Network Adapter** page appears.

7. Go to **Network** and select the virtual machine that you want to connect to.

8. If you want to configure a static MAC address or virtual LAN identifier, specify an address or identifier.

9. Click **OK**.

Tips for Hyper-V Security

The following tips can help strengthen Hyper-V security:

- Run the server core in the parent partition.
- Uninstall the VM additions while moving VMs from the virtual server to Hyper-V.
- Use two physical adapters in the host; one for host management and another for iSCSI.
- Connect the host to the back-end management networks and connect the guests to the front-end production networks.

Hyper-V Security Best Practices

- *Use a Server Core installation of Windows Server 2008 for the management operating system*: A Server Core installation provides the smallest attack surface and reduces the number of patches, updates, and restarts required for maintenance.

- *Do not run any applications in the management operating system—run all applications on virtual machines*: By keeping the management operating system free of applications and running a Windows Server 2008 core installation, fewer updates to the management operating system will be needed because nothing requires software updates except the Server Core installation, the Hyper-V service components, and the hypervisor.

- *Use the security level of the virtual machines to determine the security level of the management operating system*: Deploy virtual machines onto virtualization servers that have similar security requirements. For example, the level of risk and effort to secure servers could be classified into three categories: "secure," "more secure," and "most secure."

- *More compliance effort and control procedures should be put into the "most secure" servers than on the "secure" servers*: This is true whether the server is physical or running on a virtual machine. If both "secure" and "most secure" virtual machines are deployed on the management operating system, then the virtualization server should be secured as the "most secure" server. Deploying virtual machines with similar security levels on a virtualization server can make management and movement of the virtual machines easier.

- *Do not give virtual machine administrators permissions on the management operating system*: According to the principle of least privilege, administrators of a virtual machine (sometimes called department administrators or delegated administrators) should be given the minimum permissions required. Managing the required permissions on all the objects associated with a virtual machine can be complex and can lead to potential security issues if not handled properly. *Role-based access control* enables the user to specify access control in terms of the organizational structure of a company by creating a new object called a role. A role is assigned to a user to perform a job function. Hyper-V uses Authorization Manager policies for role based access control.

- *Ensure that virtual machines are fully updated before they are deployed in a production environment*: Because virtual machines are portable and quicker to deploy than physical machines, there is a greater risk that a virtual machine that is not fully updated or patched might be deployed. To manage this risk effectively, use the same methods and procedures to update both virtual machines and physical servers. For example, if automatic updates are allowed using Windows Update, Microsoft System Center Configuration Manager, or another software distribution method, ensure that virtual machines are updated and/or patched before they are deployed.

- *Maintenance hosts and quick migration in Hyper-V can be used to update virtual machines*: A maintenance host is a host computer that can be dedicated to patching the stored resources and for staging virtual machines before they are moved into a production environment. Ensure integration services are installed on the virtual machines. The accuracy of time stamps and audit log entries is important for computer forensics and compliance. Integration services ensure that time is synchronized between virtual machines and the management operating system. This synchronization makes sure that time is consistent with the physical location of the virtual machine in the event that virtual machines are migrated between data centers in different time zones or virtual machines are restored from previous snapshots.

- *Use a dedicated network adapter for the management operating system of the virtualization server*: By default, no virtual networking is configured for the management operating system. Use a dedicated network adapter for managing the server running Hyper-V and do not expose it to untrusted network traffic. Do not allow virtual machines to use this network adapter. Use one or more different dedicated network adapters for virtual machine networking. This allows the user to apply different levels of networking security policy and configuration for the virtual machines. For example, networking can be configured so that the virtual machines have different networking access than the management operating system, including the use of virtual local area networks (VLANs), Internet Protocol Security (IPsec), Network Access Protection (NAP), and Microsoft Forefront Threat Management Gateway.

- *Use BitLocker Drive Encryption to protect resources*: BitLocker Drive Encryption works with features in the server hardware and firmware to provide secure operating system boot and disk drive encryption, even when the server is not powered on. This helps protect data if a disk is stolen and mounted on another computer for data mining. BitLocker Drive Encryption also helps protect data if an attacker uses a different operating system or runs a software hacking tool to access a disk.

- *Losing a physical disk is a more significant risk in scenarios with small and medium businesses, as well as remote offices, where the physical security of the server may not be as rigorous as in an enterprise data center*: However, using BitLocker Drive Encryption makes sense for all computers. Use BitLocker Drive Encryption on all volumes that store virtual machine files. This includes virtual hard disks, configuration files, snapshots, and any virtual machine resources, such as ISO images and virtual floppy disks. For a higher level of security that includes secure startup, BitLocker Drive Encryption requires Trusted Platform Module (TPM) hardware.

- *Disable virtualization BIOS settings when they are not required*: When a server is no longer being used for virtualization, for example, in a test or development scenario, turn off the hardware-assisted virtualization BIOS settings that were required for Hyper-V. For instructions on disabling these settings, consult the hardware manufacturer.

Chapter Summary

- Microsoft virtualization technologies can be used to manage physical and virtual IT resources across multiple operating systems and hypervisors, from the data center to the desktop.

- With Hyper-V, the user can run multiple operating systems, such as Windows, Linux, and others, on a single server.

- A hypervisor is a thin layer of software that can run multiple operating systems on a single server simultaneously.

- The virtualization stack is a group of software components that cooperate to support virtual machines.

- Hyper-V supports isolation using partitions in which the operating system is running.

- Hyper-V uses its dispersed clustering capabilities to provide solutions during disaster recovery within IT environments and across data centers.

- A Server Core installation provides the smallest attack surface and reduces the number of patches, updates, and restarts required for maintenance.

- By keeping the management operating system free of applications and running a Windows Server 2008 core installation, fewer updates to the management operating system will be needed because nothing requires software updates except the Server Core installation, the Hyper-V service components, and the hypervisor.

Review Questions

1. Explain Hyper-V technology.

   _____

   _____

   _____

   _____

2. List the various steps involved in the installation of Hyper-V.

   _____

   _____

   _____

   _____

3. How are Hyper-V server virtual networks created and configured?

   _____

   _____

   _____

   _____

4. List the security assumptions that are necessary to design a Hyper-V installation.

   _____

   _____

   _____

   _____

5. List the factors to be considered while securing Hyper-V.

   _____

   _____

   _____

   _____

6. List the advantages of business continuity solutions.

   _____

   _____

   _____

   _____

7. What is the virtualization stack?

   _____

   _____

   _____

   _____

8. What kind of strategies should be used to strengthen Hyper-V security?

   _____

   _____

   _____

   _____

9. How can businesses mitigate the risks of losing a physical disk?

_____

_____

_____

_____

10. What is BitLocker Drive Encryption?

_____

_____

_____

_____

Hands-On Projects

1. Navigate to Chapter 3 of the Student Resource Center. Open Hyper-V_ProductOverview_v1_2.pdf and read the following topics:
   - Hyper-V Overview
   - Hyper-V as Part of Microsoft's Datacenter-to-desktop Virtualization Strategy
   - Addressing Key Business Needs

2. Navigate to Chapter 3 of the Student Resource Center. Open Microsoft Virtual Server 2005.pdf and read the following topics:
   - What Is Virtualization, and When Should You Use It?
   - What Virtualization Tools Are Available?
   - How Does Virtualization Work?

3. Navigate to Chapter 3 of the Student Resource Center. Open Virtualization with Windows Server 2008 Hyper-V.pdf and read the following topics:
   - Virtualization 2010
   - Server Virtualization Usage Scenarios
   - Hyper-V Architecture

## Chapter 4

Citrix Xen Virtualization

Objectives

After completing this chapter, you should be able to:

- Use Citrix XenServer
- Install the XenServer host
- Install the XenCenter administrator console

Key Terms

Virtualization stack   a set of software components that work together to support virtual machines

Introduction to Citrix Xen Virtualization

Citrix provides software with virtualization management and automation capabilities, such as Citrix Essentials, for its free XenServer. Citrix virtualization provides several benefits to organizations that have already deployed a virtual infrastructure, including:

- Centralized data management and maintenance
- Monitoring and access control
- Protecting data from theft, destruction, and attacks
- Reducing the physical deployment to users' devices
- Minimizing the impact of device and network variables
- Managing access from unmanaged devices
- Significantly lower total cost of ownership (TCO)
- Managed performance for the best user experience
- Delivery to any device over any connection

This chapter teaches you how to effectively use Citrix Xen virtualization with the XenServer and XenClient programs.

Virtual Server Product Comparison

Table 4-1 shows a comparison of VMware/EMC, Microsoft, and Xen virtual servers.

	VMware/EMC	**Microsoft**	**Xen**
Free server product	VMware Server	Virtual Server 2005 R2	XenExpress
Paid server products	Infrastructure v3 (Starter, Standard, and Enterprise)	None	XenServer and Enterprise
Host OS	Server: Windows Server 2003, various Linux	Windows Server 2003 SP1, XP Pro SP2 (for testing purposes only)	Bare metal
	Infra v3: bare metal		
Support resources	High	Medium	Medium
Management tools	Virtual Center VMotion migration tool	System Center VM Manager	Administrator Console
Advantages	Widest selection of prebuilt appliances, widest selection of guest OS support, wizards to help with installation	Can run on the Internet Explorer browser with Internet access; inexpensive, easy cloning of VM images	Open-source solution that doesn't require a host OS
Disadvantages	Confusing array of pricing and configuration options	Only four "virtual hard disk" prebuilt appliances of Microsoft server products	Limited hardware support, limited Windows guest-OS support

Table 4-1 Different virtual servers are useful in different situations

Citrix XenServer 5

Citrix XenServer is a free virtualization platform based on the open-source Xen hypervisor. It includes Xen-Center, a multiserver management console with core management features such as multiserver management, virtual machine (VM) templates, snapshots, shared storage support, resource pools, and XenMotion live migration. In addition, Citrix offers advanced management capabilities with Citrix Essentials for the XenServer product line. Citrix Essentials for XenServer is available in two editions: Enterprise and Platinum.

XenServer provides data centers with faster application delivery, higher availability, and better resource usage. It uses the Xen hypervisor to virtualize each server on which XenServer is installed. This allows the hypervisor to host multiple virtual machines at the same time. It uses shared storage architecture and resource clustering technology to combine multiple Xen-enabled servers into a resource pool. This reduces complexity and cost while simplifying the implementation and utility of a virtualized data center environment.

Features of XenServer include the following:

- Live migration
- Shared storage support
- Multiserver management plus P2V (physical-to-virtual) and V2V (virtual-to-virtual) conversion tools
- Near-native bare-metal performance
- Open storage APIs allow for advanced functions such as snapshotting, cloning, replication, deduplication, and provisioning in existing storage systems
- Dynamic provisioning services for on-demand deployment of workloads to any combination of virtual machines or physical servers from a single image
- High availability, thanks to automatic restart and intelligent placement of virtual machines
- XenMotion's live migration functionality can migrate the virtual machines to other physical hardware with zero downtime, allowing the machines to be patched and updated without the users' knowledge

Figure 4-1 shows some of XenServer's features, compared to those of VMware ESXi.

Features included at no cost	Citrix XenServer	VMware ESXi
Bare-metal hypervisor	64-bit	32-bit
Max virtual CPUs	8	4
Windows® and Linux guests	✔	✔
Unlimited servers, VMs, memory	✔	✔
P2V & V2V conversion	✔	✔
Shared SAN and NAS storage	✔	✔
Centralized multi-server management	✔	
Resilient distributed management architecture	✔	
Live motion	✔	
Shared VM template library	✔	
Centralized configuration management	✔	
Virtual infrastructure patch management	✔	
Intelligent initial VM placement	✔	
Intelligent server maintenance mode	✔	
Fine-grained CPU resource controls	✔	
Hot-swappable disks and NICs	✔	

Figure 4-1   XenServer has many useful features at no extra cost.

XenServer Editions

XenServer comes in the following three editions, shown in Figure 4-2:

- *Citrix XenServer Enterprise Edition*: Enterprise Edition is used by larger enterprises and supports advanced features, such as live migration and shared storage resources.
- *Citrix XenServer Standard Edition*: Standard Edition is used by Windows IT professionals. It allows up to eight VMs at the same time on a dual-socket server with up to 8 GB of memory. It does not support any Linux guests, but it supports all Windows guests. This edition can manage multiple servers from the management console.
- *Citrix XenServer Express Edition*: Express Edition is used by IT developers. It allows up to four VMs at the same time on a dual-socket server with 4 GB of memory. It supports Linux P2V conversions and Windows guests. This edition can only manage a single server.

XenServer Infrastructure

A *virtualization stack* is a set of software components that work together to support virtual machines. The following are the components of XenServer's infrastructure:

- Virtual machine (VM) hosting provides a dedicated server and operating system installation running on a redundant hardware platform.
- The guest operating system communicates with the hypervisor via hypercalls.
- Device driver architecture comprises two cooperating drivers:
  - The front-end driver runs in an unprivileged domain
  - The back-end driver runs in a domain with real access to the real hardware
- The Xen hypercall API allows customers to achieve dynamic IT environments by using virtual environments.

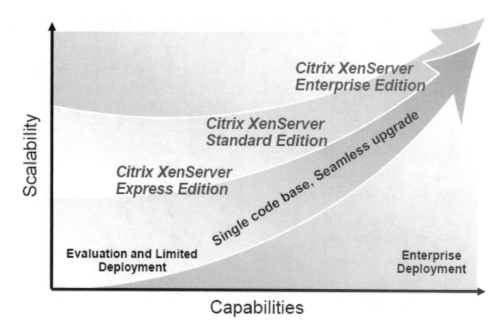

Figure 4-2 XenServer has three editions, depending on the user's needs.

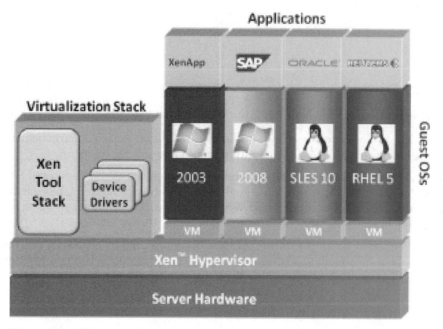

Figure 4-3 This represents XenServer's infrastructure.

- The Xen hypervisor includes control domain performance tuning, updated paravirtualization drivers, and VHD performance tuning.
- Server hardware allows a physical server to support multiple operating systems simultaneously.
- An application virtualization solution delivers applications to any device or operating system.

Figure 4-3 shows the infrastructure of XenServer, while Figure 4-4 shows the XenServer resource pool.

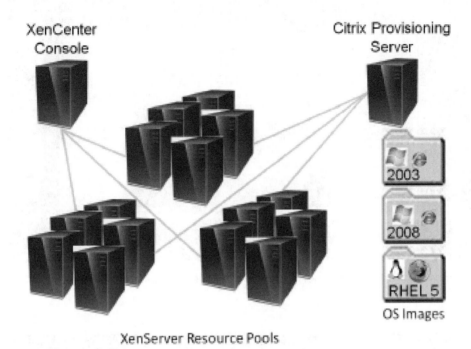

Figure 4-4   This shows XenServer's resource pool.

Installing XenServer Host

The XenServer host consists of a Xen-enabled Linux operating system, a management agent, VM templates, and a local storage repository reserved for VMs. It must be installed on a dedicated 64-bit x86 server. It is not supported in a dual-boot configuration with any other operating system. The XenServer host can be installed from its installation CDs or from a network-accessible TFTP server to boot from via Preboot Execution Environment (PXE). The major components of Citrix XenServer are packaged as ISO images, which must be burned onto CDs before use.

To install XenServer, a user follows these steps:

1. From the **Welcome to XenServer** screen, press Enter to install or upgrade Citrix XenServer.

2. Select the keyboard layout from the **Select Keymap** screen and select **OK** to continue.

3. Select **Install or Upgrade XenServer Host** from the next **Welcome to XenServer** screen and select **OK** to continue.

4. Select **OK** to confirm data backup.

5. Select **Accept EULA** to accept the End User License Agreement.

6. Select **OK** to continue installation. Note that if the server does not support the latest hardware virtualization techniques from Intel or AMD, the screen shown in Figure 4-5 will appear. The server will still be able to run various Linux distributions as virtual machines.

7. Select the installation source and select **OK** to continue.

8. Select **Yes** to install the Linux Pack from the second downloaded CD.

9. To save time, select **Skip verification** and select **OK** to continue.

10. Enter the desired root password in both fields and select **OK**. This password can also be used when connecting to the XenServer host from XenCenter.

11. Enter the network configuration in the **Networking** screen and select **OK** to continue.

12. Enter the hostname and DNS configuration and select **OK** to continue.

13. Select the host's region and a city and select **OK** to continue.

14. Select **Using NTP** in the **System Time** screen.

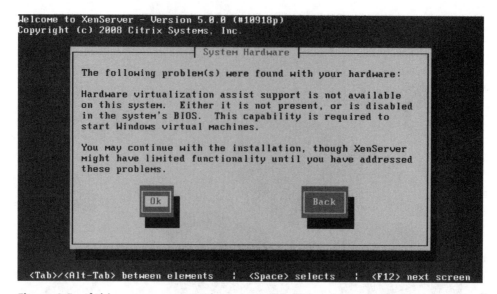

Figure 4-5   If this screen appears, the server will still be able to run many Linux distributions.

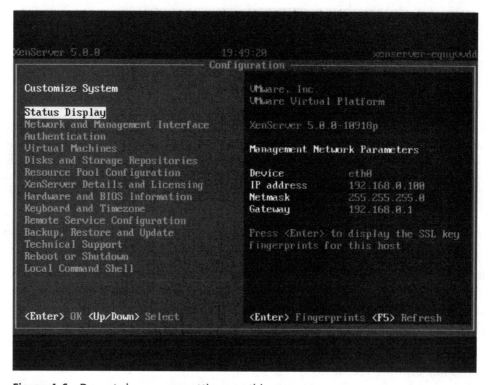

Figure 4-6   Do not change any settings on this menu.

15. Enter details of the NTP servers to be used and select **OK** to continue.
16. Select **Install XenServer** to begin the installation to the hard drive.
17. When prompted, insert the second CD and select **OK** to continue.
18. To save time, select **Use media** to skip the verification test of the second CD.
19. When prompted, click **OK** to reboot the system.
20. When rebooting, the Configuration menu shown in Figure 4-6 is displayed. Do not change any settings; just continue.

XenCenter

XenCenter is a Windows client application for connecting to a XenServer host through the network. It cannot run on the same machine as the XenServer host. It requires .NET framework version 2.0 or above.

XenCenter administrators can:

- Create, start, stop, reboot, suspend, resume, migrate, and uninstall virtual machines
- Securely reboot and shut down physical servers from any location

The following are some of the features of XenCenter:

- *Powerful, self-healing management architecture*: XenCenter distributes management data across servers in a resource pool to ensure that there can be no single point of management failure. If a management server fails, any other server in the pool can take over the management role.
- *Searching, sorting, and tagging*: User-defined grouping and metadata tags allow simple and powerful searching and sorting capabilities across virtual machines, hosts, and resource pools based on custom fields. This helps administrators identify and manage the virtual infrastructure.
- *Performance monitoring and trending*: XenCenter includes performance monitoring, reporting, and alerting dashboards. These make it easy for IT professionals to see both real-time and historical views of virtual machines and physical host performance over long periods of time with virtually no storage or performance overhead.
- *Physical to virtual*: The XenConvert feature can move existing physical server workloads to the XenServer virtual infrastructure in practically no time. Tools are also available to convert other virtual machines to run on XenServer.

Configuring the XenCenter Administrator Console

To install the XenCenter administrator console, users insert the installation CD into a Windows system and follow the on-screen instructions. The users then start XenCenter and configure it by following these steps:

1. On the Home tab, click on **Add your XenServer** and enter the hostname/IP address, the username (*root*), and the root password. Click the **Connect** button.
2. Check the **Save and restore connection state on startup** check box in the **Save and Restore Connection State** dialog box and click the **OK** button.
3. Click the **New VM** button, shown in Figure 4-7.
4. Select the guest operating system in the New VM wizard and click the **Next** button.
5. Enter a name and description for the new VM and then click the **Next** button.
6. Enter the number of virtual CPUs (vCPUs) and initial memory for the new VM, and click the **Next** button.
7. Specify the virtual disks for the new VM and then click the **Next** button.
8. Add or remove the virtual network interfaces for the new VM and then click the **Next** button.
9. Check the **Start VM automatically** check box and click the **Finish** button. Once the VM is created, it will launch automatically and be ready to use immediately.

Xen Security

When configuring a Xen system, administrators must make sure that the management domain (Domain0) is deployed securely. If the management domain is compromised, the other domains become vulnerable. Administrators should run only required services in the management partition and use a firewall with default-reject rules to prevent attacks on the management domain. Users should not be allowed to access Domain0.

To secure a Xen system, administrators must do the following:

- Apply the latest patches
- Close unnecessary ports
- Audit for unusual or suspicious behaviour

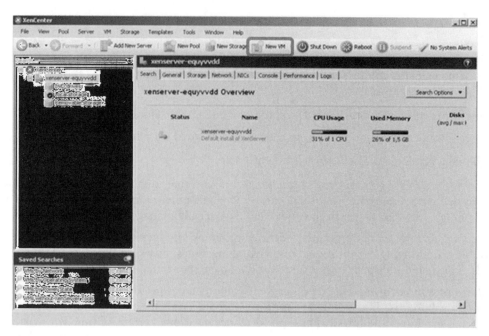

Figure 4-7   Click the **New VM** button.

To enhance the security of a Xen system, administrators should consider the following:

- Separate system functionality into special-purpose virtual machines
  - Special-purpose virtual machines increase security and restrict access to resources and other machines.
  - Administrators use special VMs to compare the security level of software and data that exist on that system.
  - Creating a VM for each service becomes a resource-intensive and potentially wasteful task.
- Create virtual network segments
  - Create virtual network segments for all internal VMs using the Web server, and use a VM as an interface with a routable IP address on the public network segment.
  - Fix a firewall or NAT VM with an interface on both network segments.
  - Xen can isolate the VMs from the public network.
  - Internal VMs require both Internet access and access to the internal file share. The VMs must contain two virtual network interfaces: one on the isolated file-share network, and the other on the internal firewalled segment.

Securely Removing Software and Services

For both security and performance, it is best to limit the software installed and running on the system. Administrators should move the unnecessary services for guest management out of Domain0 and into guest VMs. Any service running in Domain0 is a possible entry point for an attack.

Acceptable installed software includes the following:

- Kernel of the OS
- User-space programs
- System services
- Network services
- Configuration files

The less software installed, the easier it is to detect problems and maintain the system.

Limiting Remote Access

It is important to restrict the access of domains running network services, because they are the primary entry point for attackers. When a service such as FTP or HTTP is compromised, migrating network services into unprivileged domains helps limit the damage to a single VM.

Administrators should monitor the outgoing network access of domains running network services. A proper backup plan can prevent intrusions or quickly restore compromised virtual machines. Any remaining open network port on Domain0 should be treated as a possible entry point and point of attack. It may be beneficial to allow console-only access to Domain0. However, in some environments console access may simply not be possible. Individual guest domains could still be remotely accessible even if the remote administration of Domain0 is disabled.

Citrix XenApp Business Continuity

Citrix XenApp business continuity and disaster recovery solutions eliminate the need to rebuild networks and desktops. Application maintenance is transparent, and there are no business issues for the end users. XenApp also eliminates the need to update the user's devices, minimizing interruptions.

Chapter Summary

- Citrix XenServer comes in three editions: Enterprise, Standard, and Express.
- XenServer is a powerful server virtualization solution that provides data centers with faster application delivery, higher availability, and better resource usage.
- XenMotion's live migration functionality can migrate virtual machines to other physical hardware with zero downtime, and it allows administrators to patch and update machines without any disruption to end users.

Review Questions

1. What are the benefits of Citrix virtualization?

   _____

   _____

   _____

   _____

2. What are the advantages of Citrix over other virtual servers?

   _____

   _____

   _____

   _____

3. What are some features of Citrix XenServer?

   _____

   _____

   _____

   _____

4. Explain the XenServer infrastructure.

_____

_____

_____

_____

5. What are some ways to secure a Xen system?

_____

_____

_____

_____

Hands-On Projects

HANDS-ON PROJECTS

1. Install Citrix XenServer and Citrix XenCenter.

   ■ Navigate to Chapter 4 of the Student Resource Center and click on link to download the Citrix XenServer and Cintrix XenCenter.

   ■ Install the Citrix XenServer and Citrix XenCenter programs using the instructions in this chapter.

2. Read about the Xen architecture.

   ■ Navigate to Chapter 4 of the Student Resource Center.

   ■ Open Xen Architecture_Q1 2008.pdf and read the content.

3. Read the XenServer Administrator's Guide.

   ■ Navigate to Chapter 4 of the Student Resource Center.

   ■ Open XenServer Administrator's Guide (reference).pdf and read the content.

4. Read about XenDesktop.

   ■ Navigate to Chapter 4 of the Student Resource Center.

   ■ Open Getting-Started-XenDesktop.pdf and read the content.

5. Read about the XenServer Software Development Kit (SDK).

   ■ Navigate to Chapter 4 of the Student Resource Center.

   ■ Open XenServer Software Development Kit Guide.pdf and read the content.

## Chapter 5

Sun Virtualization

Objectives

After completing this chapter, you should be able to:

- Discuss Sun virtualization products and services
- Install and configure the xVM Ops Center
- Administer an xVM Ops Center
- Install VirtualBox on Windows hosts
- Install VirtualBox on Mac hosts
- Discuss Sun Virtual Desktop Infrastructure Software

Key Terms

Disconnected mode architecture   a Sun xVM architecture that does not connect to any other system via any network

Enterprise controller   a central server for Sun virtualization that manages the connected systems using a user-friendly browser interface

Proxy controller   proxy used by the enterprise controller to handle the managed systems in the Sun xVM Ops Center

Sun xVM Ops Center   a data center life-cycle management tool that enables the user to discover, patch, manage, and monitor the assets in one or more data centers from a single console

Introduction to Sun Virtualization

Virtualization is a framework or methodology that divides the resources of a computer into multiple execution environments. It is rapidly being deployed in server, storage, networking, and client environments. Sun offers a complete desktop-to-data-center virtualization product portfolio and a comprehensive set of virtualization service offerings to help customers deploy new services quickly,

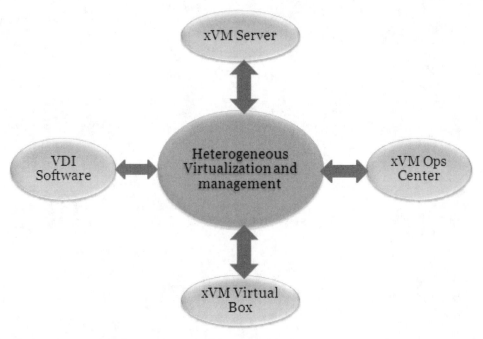

Figure 5-1 Sun has four main virtualization products.

maximize the utilization of the system's resources, and monitor and manage the virtualized environments. Sun offers the following virtualization products and services:

- Desktop virtualization
- Server virtualization
- Storage virtualization
- Virtualization management
- Virtualization services

Sun offers the following four virtualization products, as shown in Figure 5-1:

- xVM Ops Center
- VDI Software
- xVM Server
- xVM VirtualBox

Sun Virtualization Features

Sun virtualization, shown in Figure 5-2, offers the following features:

- Hard partitions
  - Remote Access Services (RAS)
  - Scalability
  - Established technology
  - Ability to run different OS versions
- Virtual machines
  - Ability to migrate an OS
  - Run different OS versions and types
  - Decouples OS and hardware versions

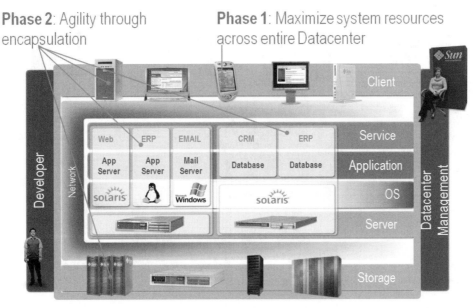

Figure 5-2   Sun virtualization provides a host of benefits.

- OS virtualization
    - Scalable; low overhead
    - One OS to manage
    - Divides system and application administration
    - Fine-grained resource management
- Resource management
    - Scalable and low overhead
    - Single OS to manage

Sun Desktop Virtualization

From an IT administrator's perspective, it is difficult to manage desktops and laptops. Virtualizing desktops can replace traditional PCs with virtual machines that can be managed from a remote and secure data center. Virtualizing desktops is similar to server virtualization.

Desktop virtualization provides the following benefits:

- Increases the desktop's life span
- Protects intellectual property and leaves no data behind
- Provides better regulatory compliance because data are not distributed
- Increases user satisfaction and retention
- Leverages thin client's benefits today while still supporting legacy applications
- Easy to implement, fast to deploy, and cheaper to manage

Sun VDI Software's open architecture allows IT departments to design a virtual desktop environment using a broad range of client devices, virtualization hosts, and virtual desktop operating systems, as shown in Figure 5-3. Sun desktop virtualization helps separate the desktop operating system and some, or all, of its applications from the underlying hardware. Each desktop instance is executed in a self-contained environment. The interaction of the individual desktop instances and the resources they use are controlled and managed by a virtualization layer.

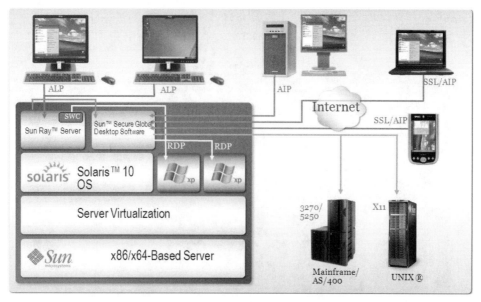

Figure 5-3 Each desktop instance is executed in a self-contained environment.

Sun xVM Ops Center

Sun xVM Ops Center is a data center life-cycle management tool that enables the user to discover, patch, manage, and monitor the assets in one or more data centers from a single console. The remote management capabilities are designed to increase availability and utilization, and minimize downtime.

The user interface displays a consolidated view of all the resources in the data center, including physical systems (x86 and SPARC), operating systems, and Solaris Containers and Zones.

The following tasks can be performed using the Sun xVM Ops Center console:

- Manage physical systems in a data center
- Provide systems with Solaris or Linux operating systems
- Automate patching and updates for Solaris and Linux operating systems
- Generate a variety of reports

The Sun xVM Ops Center console uses a three-tiered architecture consisting of the following components:

- *Enterprise controller*: The enterprise controller is a central server that manages the connected systems using a user-friendly browser interface. It connects to managed systems through proxy controllers. Here, the enterprise controller has the flexibility to connect with the Internet to download patch information from Sun Knowledge Services and to download patches from software vendors such as SuSE, Solaris, and Linux.

- *Proxy controller*: The enterprise controller requires one or more proxies for handling the managed systems. Proxies directly interact with the managed systems and thus increase the scalability of the enterprise controller.

- *Agent*: An agent is deployed for patch management. It helps an enterprise controller to identify hardware. Once the agent is installed, it appears on the managed gear section of the Navigation panel.

- *Management network*: Through the management network, the user can remotely control physical systems managed by Sun xVM Ops Center. With the help of this network, the user can perform the following functions:
  - Power on or off
  - Conduct a firmware update and OS provisioning
  - Discover boot device information and parameters

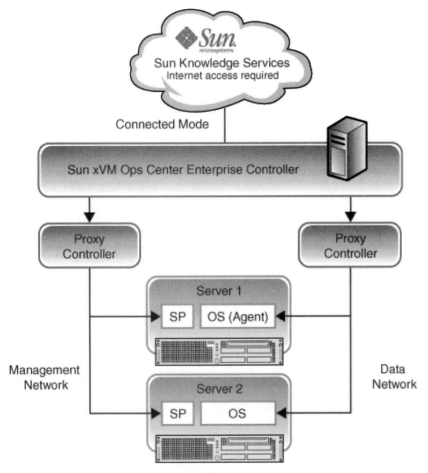

Figure 5-4   The Sun xVM Ops Center normally functions in connected mode.

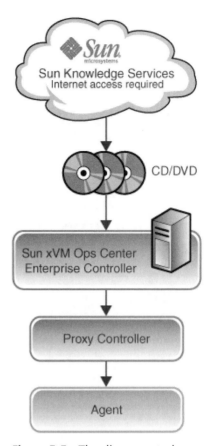

Figure 5-5   The disconnected mode architecture is isolated from other systems on the network.

- *Data network*: In the data network, the operating systems running on the managed systems are separately managed. The user requires a separate proxy in order to manage this network. It can perform the following functions:
  - Provisioning, patching, and rebooting operating systems
  - Providing operating system information (type and version) and zone-related information (representation of global and nonglobal zones)
  - Listing information on CPU, memory, and network usage

Connected and Disconnected Modes of Architecture

The Sun xVM Ops Center normally functions in the connected mode. Figure 5-4 shows this type of architecture.

The ***disconnected mode architecture*** enables the user to access Sun xVM Ops Center in a secured environment. The term *disconnected* makes it clear that this architecture does not connect with any other system via any network (such as the Internet), as shown in Figure 5-5. Sun architecture provides the flexibility to switch from the connected mode to the disconnected mode, depending upon the users' requirements.

Sun xVM Ops Center Port Requirements

Figure 5-6 lists various Sun xVM Ops Center communication requirements. In addition, depending on the environment that is being managed, the enterprise controller has to browse various vendor sites to download patches or other knowledge. Figure 5-7 shows the requirements and data flow for the xVM Ops Center.

At least one proxy controller is mandatory. It may be installed during the enterprise controller installation on the same machine as the enterprise controller, or on a separate server.

Communication	Port and Protocol	Purpose
Browser to Satellite	HTTPS, TCP 9443	Web interface
Browser to Satellite	HTTPS, TCP 80	Redirect to port 9443
Proxy to Satellite	HTTPS, TCP 443	• Proxy push of inventory data to server • Proxy pull of jobs, update, agent, and OS images
Proxy to Systems	• FTP, TCP 21 • SSH, TCP 22 • Telnet, TCP 23 • DHCP, UDP 67, 68 • SNMP, UDP 161, 162 • IPMI, TCP+UDP 623 • Service Tags UDP 6481	• Discovery • Bare metal provisioning • System management • Monitoring
Agent to Proxy	HTTPS, TCP 21165	• Agent push of inventory data to proxy • Agent pull of jobs
Agent to Proxy	HTTPS, TCP 8002	• Agent push of inventory data to proxy • Agent pull of jobs
OS to Proxy	HTTPS, TCP 8004	• OS provisioning completion status • Linux provisioning • Download the agent tar file after OS provisioning • Upload status messages to the satellite server about failed agent installations

Figure 5-6 The Ops Center requires different ports for each aspect of its architecture.

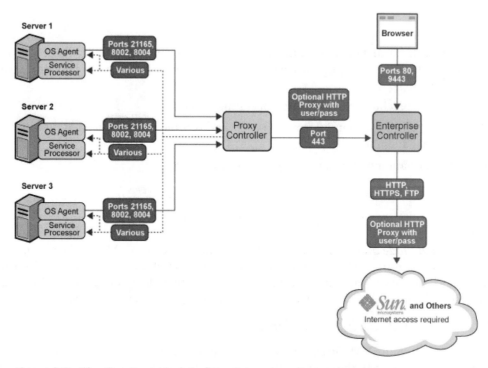

Figure 5-7 The Ops Center's data flow determines the ports required.

Enterprise Controller Administration

The enterprise controller is the core of Sun xVM Ops Center. It generates the browser interface, routes commands from the user to the proper proxy controller, and communicates with Sun and other external data sources. Enterprise controller administration enables the following functions:

- Unconfiguring an enterprise controller
- Updating Sun xVM Ops Center
- Authentications
- Connection mode
- Viewing service status
- Viewing agent controllers
- Updating agent controllers
- Viewing logs

xVM Ops Center Installation and Configuration

Figure 5-8 shows the details for preparing a site for xVM Ops Center installation and configuration.

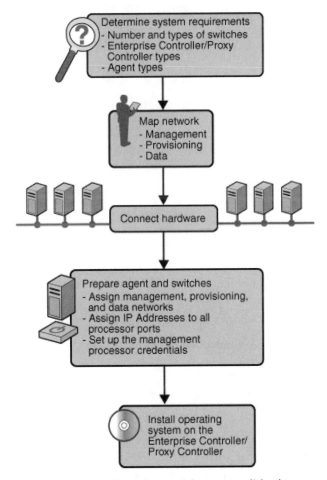

Figure 5-8 Specific tasks must be accomplished to prepare a site for Ops Center installation.

Component	Recommended Value
Memory	4 GB Available RAM

Hard Disk	74 GB minimum free space available, including:
	  70 GB free in /var/opt/sun/xvm for Sun xVM Ops Center data
	  4 GB free in /var/opt/sun/xvm/images/os for each OS image stored for use in OS
	    provisioning
	  2 GB free in /opt and /var/tmp for xVM software installation

Available Swap Space	4 GB minimum
Operating System	Sun xVM Ops Center 2.0 Proxy Controllers require Solaris 10 (x64 or SPARC), or Red Hat Enterprise Linux (RHEL) 5.0
Processor	AMD Opteron and Intel Xeon: 1 sockets; 2 or more cores UltraSPARC T1/T2: 1 socket; 1 or more cores UltraSPARC IV+/IV: 1 sockets UltraSPARC IIIi: 1 sockets
Network Connection	At least one Network Interface Card (NIC)

Figure 5-9 Ops Center installation has specific prerequisites.

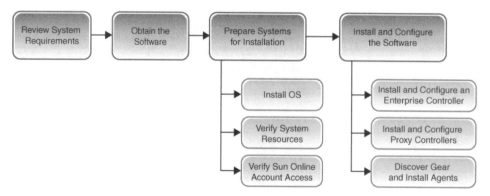

Figure 5-10 Ops Center installation and configuration should follow this flowchart.

The system requirements shown in Figure 5-9 should be considered when installing the following Sun xVM Ops Center components:

- Sun xVM Ops Center Enterprise Controller software
- Sun xVM Ops Center Proxy Controller software

Ops Center Installation

Figure 5-10 shows the installation and configuration flow for Ops Center. The following steps will install the Sun xVM Ops Center:

1. Review the system's requirements.

2. Obtain the Sun xVM Ops Center software.

3. Prepare a set of systems for software installation. This involves the following steps:

 - Install an operating system.
 - Verify the system's resources.
 - Verify Sun's online account access.

4. Install a Sun xVM Ops Center enterprise controller and proxy controller, discover gear, and install agents. Use the following steps to accomplish this:
   - Install and configure an enterprise controller.
   - Install and configure a proxy controller.
   - Discover gear and install agents.

Enterprise Controller Installation

The following steps should be used to install a Sun xVM Ops Center enterprise controller:

1. Create a temporary directory on the system. Copy or move the appropriate archive from Sun to the temporary directory, as shown in Figure 5-11.
2. Change to the directory where the installation archive is located on the system. Extract the compressed (.tar) archive. List the contents of the temporary directory, as shown in Figure 5-12.
3. Change the directory to the location where the install script resides:
   - Run the install script.
   - Each installation archive contains an install script that is appropriate for its intended operating system and platform.
   - The screen clears and the install script displays a list of the installation tasks.
4. The install script checks for prerequisites and reports needed updates to the user. Once the prerequisites are met, the installation process is successful. If the prerequisites are not met, use the following steps:
   - Enter **t** to try again.
   - Enter **c** to continue, thus ignoring the warning.
   - Enter **x** to exit from the install script.

```
# mkdir /var/tmp/xVM
# cp xVM-Ops-Center-sol-sparc-GA-2-0.tar.gz /var/tmp/xVM
```

Figure 5-11   Copy or move the appropriate archive from Sun to the temporary directory.

```
# cd /var/tmp/xVM
# gzcat xVM-Ops-Center-sol-sparc-GA-2-0.tar.gz | tar xf -
# ls Copyright
install
license
LICENSE_MULTILANGUAGE.pdf
Linux_i686
SunOS_i386
SunOS_sparc
THIRDPARTYLICENSEREADME
xVM-Ops-Center-sol-sparc-GA-2-0.tar.gz
#
```

Figure 5-12   List the contents of the temporary directory.

Enterprise Controller Software Configuration

For complete installation of Sun xVM Ops Center, installation and configuration of the Enterprise Controller software is a prerequisite. The following steps are used to configure a Sun xVM Ops Center enterprise controller:

1. Launch a Web browser.
2. Connect to the following URL:
   - https://<system>:9443.
   - Replace <system> with the IP address or hostname of the system.
3. Accept any certificates that are presented (login page will be displayed).
4. Enter the name and password of the root user, or equivalent role, on the system. The **Introduction** panel of the Enterprise Controller Configuration wizard is then displayed.
5. To display the **Enterprise Controller** panel, click **Next**.
6. Provide the information in Figure 5-13.
7. Click **Next** to display the **HTTP Proxy** panel.
   - This panel enables the user to specify information about an HTTP proxy.
   - Provide the information from Figure 5-14.
8. Click **Next** to display the **Registration** panel.
9. The **Register Enterprise Controller with Sun Datacenter** check box allows the user to choose registration for online services. The user's selection in this panel determines what panels the Enterprise Controller Configuration wizard will display next. If the user wants to register the enterprise controller with Sun Inventory online service, then select **Register Enterprise Controller with Sun Datacenter**.
10. Click **Next**.

- **Name**
  Enter the name that you want to use to identify this Sun xVM Ops Center Enterprise Controller. The name that you specify here might differ from the host name of the Sun xVM Ops Center Enterprise Controller.
- **Description**
  Enter a brief description of the Sun xVM Ops Center Enterprise Controller.
- **Network Location**
  Enter the fully qualified host name of the Sun xVM Ops Center Enterprise Controller.
- **Use an alternative user as Administrative User instead of the currently logged in privileged user.**
  If you want to use an administrative user other than the root user on the Enterprise Controller, select this option. This option enables the Administrative User and Password fields in this panel. Choosing to use an alternative administrative user causes Sun xVM Ops Center to not accept root as a valid administrative user.
- **Administrative User**
  If you chose to use an alternative administrative user, enter the name of the user that will administer this Sun xVM Ops Center Enterprise Controller. This user account must exist on the Enterprise Controller.
- **Password**
  Enter the password for the user name that you specified in the Administrative User field.

Figure 5-13 Provide this information in Step 6.

- **Server**
  Enter the host name of the system that acts as the HTTP proxy.
- **Port**
  Enter the port of the HTTP proxy.
- **User**
  If the proxy requires authentication, enter the user name to use.
- **Password**
  If the proxy requires authentication, enter the password associated with the user name that you entered in the User field.

Figure 5-14 Step 7 requires this information.

```
# svcs '*scn*' '*common*'
STATE STIME FMRI
disabled 22:48:25  svc:/application/scn/update-agent:default
disabled 22:53:34  svc:/application/management/common-agent-container-1:default
disabled 22:53:39  svc:/application/management/common-agent-container-1:scn-proxy
disabled 22:55:51  svc:/application/scn/proxy-enable:default
disabled 22:55:55  svc:/application/scn/dhcpd:default
offline  22:55:53  svc:/application/scn/proxy-available:default
offline  22:55:59  svc:/application/scn/uce-proxy:default
```

Figure 5-15   The installed services should include those listed here.

Proxy Controller Software Installation

1. Use the following steps to create a temporary directory on the system:
   - Copy or move the appropriate archive for the system from the delivery media to the temporary directory created.
   - Use the same archive version as the one used to install the Sun xVM Ops Center enterprise controller.
2. Extract the compressed .tar archive.
3. Change the directory to the place where the install script resides, and run the install script with the -p option. The -p option causes the install script to install the Sun xVM Ops Center proxy-related components.
   - When prompted, accept the license agreement to continue with the installation.
   - Each installation archive contains an install script that is only appropriate for its intended OS and platform.
4. To verify the installation on Solaris systems, list the Sun xVM Ops Center services installed by the install script. Check for services with scn and common FMRI names. The list should include the services listed in Figure 5-15.

Proxy Controller Configuration

The following steps are used to configure the Sun xVM Ops Center proxy controller:

1. Create a temporary directory to hold the password file that will be created in this procedure.
2. Create an empty file named mypasswd in this directory, and set its permission mode to 400.
3. Edit the mypasswd file so that it contains the password of the user that was designated as the administrator of the Sun xVM Ops Center enterprise controller.
4. Use the proxyadm command to associate the proxy controller with the enterprise controller. The following options can be used:
   - -*s*: Specifies the hostname of the enterprise controller
   - -*u*: Specifies the user that was designated as the administrator of the enterprise controller
   - -*p*: Specifies the absolute pathname of the file that contains the password for the user specified with the -u option
5. Accept any certificates presented.
6. Use the proxyadm command to start proxy controller services.
7. Use the svcs command to check for services with scn and common FMRI names. The list should include the services indicated in Figure 5-16.
8. Run the **s-console list-connections** command to verify the connection has been established for the proxy controller configuration.

```
# svcs '*scn*' '*common*'
STATE STIME FMRI
disabled 0:13:47 svc:/application/scn/update-agent:default
disabled 0:18:13 svc:/application/management/common-agent-container-1:default
disabled 0:20:32 svc:/application/scn/dhcpd:default
online 1:05:54 svc:/application/scn/proxy-enable:default
online 1:06:08 svc:/application/scn/uce-proxy:default
online 1:08:05 svc:/application/management/common-agent-container-1:scn-proxy
online 1:08:05 svc:/application/scn/proxy-available:default
#
```

Figure 5-16   The listed services should include those listed here.

Ops Center Agent Installation

1. On the Sun xVM Ops Center enterprise controller, change to the directory that contains the agent installation archives.
2. Identify the agent archive appropriate for the system.
3. On the target system where the agent is to be installed, create a temporary directory.
4. Use scp or ftp to transfer the correct agent archive from the server to the temporary directory on the target system. Respond to any authentication or confirmation prompts.
5. On the target system, change to the temporary directory.
6. Unzip or extract the agent archive.
7. Run the install script in the SunConnectionAgent directory.
8. Create an empty file named mypasswd in the temporary directory, and set its permission mode to 400.
9. Edit the mypasswd file so that it contains the password for the administrative user that exists on the enterprise controller.
10. Use the agentadm command to associate the Sun xVM Ops Center agent with an xVM Ops Center proxy controller.
11. If a connection cannot be registered and an error message is obtained from the agentadm command, use agentadm to unconfigure the agent.

Sun xVM Ops Center Updating

Updating is necessary to ensure network security. The following steps are used to update Sun xVM Ops Center:

1. Go to the **Administration** section of the Navigation panel and click on the enterprise controller.
2. Click **Sun xVM Ops Center Updates**. A wizard for Sun xVM Ops Center updates is displayed.
3. Click **Show details** to view more information about updates (optional step).
4. Select **Update** and click **Next**. The license page is displayed.
5. Read and accept the license. The summary page is displayed.
6. Click **Finish**.

Editing Authentications

Authentication is one of the most important security concerns. The following steps should be used to edit authentications:

1. Go to the **Administration** section of the **Navigation panel** and click on the enterprise controller.
2. Click **Edit Authentications**. A window to edit authentications is displayed.
3. Click on a description field to add a new authentication: enter the username and password for each authentication.
4. Click **Submit**.

Switching Between Connected and Disconnected Modes

Sun xVM Ops Center operates in two modes: connected and disconnected. The connected mode of operation allows Ops Center to connect and communicate with Sun and various other vendors in order to gather updates as well as patch information, while Ops Center in disconnected mode works autonomously. The following steps will switch the Sun xVM Ops Center to the desired mode:

1. Go to the **Administration** section of the **Navigation panel** and click on the enterprise controller.
2. Click **Setup Connection Mode.**
3. To switch to **disconnected** mode:
   - Enter the absolute path of the knowledge base bundle to be used.
   - Click **Load Bundle.**
4. Click either **Switch to Disconnected Mode** or **Switch to Connected Mode.**

Viewing Service Status

The following steps should be followed to view the service status:

1. Go to the **Administration** section of the **Navigation panel** and click on the enterprise controller.
2. Click the **Status** tab: the service status will be displayed.

Viewing Agent Controllers

Agent controllers are installed on the systems managed by Ops Center. The following steps can be used to view agent controllers:

1. Go to the **Administration** section of the **Navigation panel** and click on the enterprise controller.
2. Click the **Agent Controllers** tab.
3. Information on the agent controllers is displayed.

Updating Agent Controllers

To take advantage of new features and be free from vulnerabilities, updating is necessary. Agent controllers can be updated remotely by using the following steps:

1. Go to the **Administration** section of the **Navigation panel** and click on the enterprise controller.
2. Click the **Agent Controllers** tab.
3. Select one or more agent controllers.
4. Click **Update** to update the agent software to the latest available version.

Viewing Logs

In order to diagnose problems and view user activities, viewing logs is essential. The following steps can be used to view logs:

1. Go to the **Administration** section of the **Navigation panel** and click on the enterprise controller.
2. Click the **Logs** tab.
3. Select a log from the drop-down list, which will contain the following logs:
   - Cacao log
   - UI log
   - DB transaction log
   - DB report log
   - Proxy log
   - Update error log

- Update channel download log
- Update channel error log

Proxy Controller Administration

Unregister a Proxy Controller via the Command Line

In Sun xVM Ops Center, the proxy controller is connected to the enterprise controller, but unregistering the proxy controller breaks its connection with the enterprise controller. The following steps will unregister a proxy controller via the command line:

1. Log in to the proxy controller via the command line.
2. Use the proxyadm command and stop subcommand to stop the proxy controller.
3. Unconfigure the proxy controller using the proxyadm command and the unconfigure subcommand.

Steps to Unregister a Proxy Controller Using the Browser User Interface

The following steps should be used to unregister a proxy controller using the browser user interface:

1. Go to the **Administration** section of the **Navigation panel** and click on the proxy controller.
2. Click **Unregister Proxy Controller**.
3. A confirmation window is displayed. Click **Yes** to confirm.

Set a Proxy Controller as Default

Setting a proxy controller as default helps Sun xVM Ops Center users complete their jobs using the default proxy controller wherever possible. The following steps can be used to set a proxy controller as default:

1. Go to the **Administration** section of the **Navigation panel** and click on the proxy controller.
2. Click **Set as Default**. A window appears, confirming that the proxy controller has been set as the default.
3. Click **OK**.

Configure DHCP Services

To support OS provisioning operations in Sun xVM Ops Center, configuring and enabling DHCP services on a proxy controller is required. The following steps will configure DHCP services:

1. Select the proxy controller to configure DHCP services for from the **Administration section**.
2. Select **DHCP Config** from the **Actions List**.
3. Provide the following information on the **DHCP configuration** window:
   - DHCP server
   - Interface
4. Click **Save Config** to save the DHCP configuration specified.
5. A warning indicates that any existing subnets in the DHCP configuration will be removed.
6. A message indicates that the DHCP configuration job has been submitted.

Monitoring a DHCP Configuration Job

The DHCP configuration action creates a task to configure DHCP services on the proxy controller. These services are available only after the job is completed successfully. The administrator can monitor the job progress by listing the job in the **Jobs** panel as follows:

1. Select the **Jobs** panel.
2. Select **All Jobs** or **In Progress** from the **Jobs** panel, and identify the DHCP configuration job from the list that is displayed.

3. Double-click the DHCP configuration job to display the **Job Details** panel that describes the job.

4. Click **Close** to dismiss the **Job Details** panel.

Configuring a Subnet

Subnets should be configured in order to use DHCP services on a proxy controller. The following steps are used to configure a subnet:

1. Go to the **Administration** section, select the proxy controller, and select the location to configure DHCP services.

2. Go to the **Actions List** and select **Subnets**.

3. After the **DHCP Subnets Configuration** dialog box is displayed, provide the following necessary information:

   - *Subnet*: To create a new subnet on the selected proxy controller, select **Create New Subnet**. If a subnet already exists, select the existing subnets from the drop-down list. Modify the subnet's configuration and click on the **Refresh** button to update the list of subnets.

   - *Subnet name*: Enter the name of the subnet to establish or modify DHCP services.

   - *Network*: Type the network address.

   - *Netmask*: Type the netmask for the network.

   - *Router IP address*: Provide the IP address of the router.

   - *Low IP address*: Enter the IP address to use as the low boundary of the IP address range that systems on this subnet will use.

   - *High IP address*: Enter the IP address to be used as the high boundary of the IP address range.

   - *Name server*: Provide the IP addresses of the DNS servers that systems will be using.

   - *Domain*: Enter DNS domain names to resolve the hostnames.

4. Click **Create** to create the subnet with the specified configuration.

Configuring External DHCP Servers

The Sun xVM Ops Center enables the use of DHCP servers that are external to proxy controllers in order to provide the DHCP services that OS provisioning operations require. Configuring external DHCP servers requires the following prerequisites:

- Establish DHCP relay or forwarding services on the network routers, switches, or systems that comprise the network.

- Use the scninstall_ext_dhcp.pl script to establish the communication channel between the external DHCP server and the proxy controller.

The scninstall_ext_dhcp.pl script enables SSH access to the DHCP server without requiring passwords.

The following steps are used to configure external DHCP servers:

1. Select the proxy controller.

2. Select **External DHCP Servers** from the **Actions List**.

3. Provide the following information on the **External DHCP Servers Configuration** dialog box:

   - *DHCP server*: Either create a new DHCP server or select an existing DHCP server from the list in order to modify its configuration.

   - *Subnet name*: Enter the name of the subnet for establishing or modifying DHCP services.

- *DHCP server*: Select either ISC or Solaris to implement either the Internet Standards Consortium (ISC) reference DHCP server or the Solaris native DHCP server.
- *DHCP server IP*: Enter the IP address of the DHCP server.
- *Network*: Enter the network address for establishing or modifying DHCP services.
- *Netmask*: Enter the netmask address for the network in order to establish or modify DHCP services.
- *Router IP address*: Enter the IP address of the router that the DHCP server assigns to systems.
- *Low IP address*: Enter the IP address to use as the low boundary of the IP address range that this DHCP server allocates to systems.
- *High IP address*: Enter the IP address to use as the high boundary of the IP address range that this DHCP server will allocate to systems.
- *Name server*: Enter the IP addresses of the DNS servers that systems use.
- *Domain*: Enter the names of the DNS domains that systems use to resolve hostnames

4. Click **Create DHCP Server** to create the DHCP server configuration specified.

Viewing a Proxy Controller's Configuration

The following aspects of a proxy controller configuration can be viewed:

- IP address
- Registration date
- Status (online or offline)
- Whether the proxy controller is default or not

The following steps can be used to view the proxy controller's configuration.

1. Go to the **Administration** section of the **Navigation panel** and click on the proxy controller.
2. Click the **Configuration** tab. The proxy controller's configuration is displayed.

Backup and Recovery

Backing Up an Enterprise Controller

The following steps can be used to back up an enterprise controller:

1. From the command line, log into the enterprise controller.
2. Use the satadm command to back up the controller.

Restoring an Enterprise Controller

Once the backup is created for an enterprise controller, the following steps can be used to restore it:

1. Restoration can be performed on a newly installed enterprise controller only prior to configuration. If backup restoration is on a new system, then the IP address, hostname, and Enterprise Controller software version of the restored system must match those of the backed-up system.
   - If backup restoration is on the same system, uninstall and then reinstall the Enterprise Controller software before restoring.
2. Install the enterprise controller.
   - Do not configure the server; the restore command will restore the configuration settings.
   - The enterprise controller version must match the version that was backed up.
3. Run the **satadm restore** command. The -i flag is required to restore the data from the backup file.
4. For an enterprise controller with a colocated proxy environment, use the Custom Discovery method to rediscover the system after running the restore command.

User and Role Management

Viewing Users and Roles

Users can be added to or deleted from the Sun xVM Ops Center from the local authentication subsystem of the enterprise controller's operating system. Here, users are assigned different sets of roles that either grant or deny access to various functions of the Ops Center. The following steps are used to view users and roles:

1. Select **Administration** from the **Navigation** panel.
2. Click either the **Users** tab or the **Roles** tab:
   - The Users tab will display the list of known users.
   - The Roles tab will display the role of any specified user and the authorizations granted by that role.

Adding a New User to Sun xVM Ops Center

The following steps are used to add a new user:

1. Select **Administration** from the **Navigation** panel.
2. Click the **Users** tab.
3. Click the **Add User** button.
4. Enter the username.
5. Click **Add User** and the new user is created.

Deleting a User from Sun xVM Ops Center

Deleting a user from Sun xVM Ops Center requires administrative privileges. The following steps should be used to delete a user:

1. Select **Administration** from the **Navigation** panel.
2. Click the **Users** tab.
3. Select the user to be deleted.
4. Click the **Delete User** button.
5. Click **Confirm** to delete the user.

Configuring a Notification File

Notification files determine what events generate notifications for a user and how those notifications are sent to the user. The following steps are used to configure a notification file:

1. Click the **Users** tab.
2. Select a user.
3. Click the **Configure Notification Profile** button.
4. Choose the event severity for which notifications are sent.
5. Choose the method for notification delivery and enter the necessary information.
6. Click **Update Notification Profile**.

Assigning a Role to a User

The following steps are used to assign a role to a user:

1. Select **Administration** from the **Navigation** panel.
2. Click the **Roles** tab and the **Roles** page will be displayed.
3. Select a user from the drop-down menu.
4. Select **Enterprise Controller, All Gear,** or a user-defined group.

5. Click **Edit Roles.**
6. Select the roles to be assigned.
7. Click **Update Role Capabilities.**

Sun xVM VirtualBox

Sun xVM VirtualBox is an x86 virtualization product. It is the only professional open-source software available under the terms of the GNU Public License (GPL). It supports and runs on Windows, Linux, Mac OS X, and OpenSolaris hosts.

It is installed on the host operating system that is currently being used. Within this application, the guest operating systems can be installed and run within their own virtual environments.

Features of Sun xVM VirtualBox

Sun xVM VirtualBox has the following features:

- Well-defined internal programming interfaces that allow users to have control over a number of interfaces at a time
- Virtual machine descriptions, such as configuration settings in XML, that are independent of the local machine
- Installs special software into Windows or Linux virtual machines in order to improve the performance of the virtual machine
- Shared folders for easy data exchange between hosts and guest virtual machines
- Virtual USB controllers that allow the user to connect USB devices to virtual machines
- Remote Desktop Protocol (RDP) support

Architecture and Prerequisites of Sun xVM VirtualBox

Figure 5-17 shows the architecture used for the Sun xVM VirtualBox.
The following prerequisites are necessary for Sun xVM VirtualBox:

- *x86 hardware*: Intel or AMD processor
- *Memory*: 512 MB of RAM

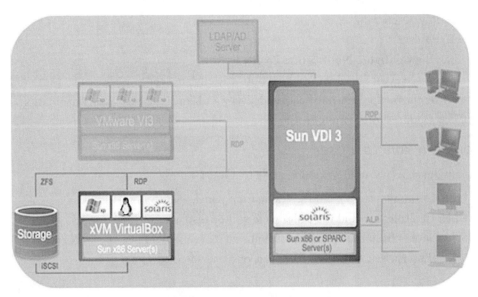

Figure 5-17   The VirtualBox architecture is shown in this diagram.

- *Hard disk space*: 30 MB
- *Host and guest operating systems*: Windows, Linux, Mac OS X, and Solaris

VirtualBox Installation on Windows Hosts

The following steps will install VirtualBox on a Windows host:

1. Double-click on the VirtualBox Microsoft Installer archive (MSI file) or enter **msiexec /i VirtualBox.msi** on the command line.

2. Create a new, empty VM for installing Windows Vista, as shown in Figure 5-18.

3. With standard settings, VirtualBox will be installed for all users on the local system. To install it for just the current user, invoke the installer as follows: **msiexec /i VirtualBox.msi ALLUSERS=2.**

VirtualBox Installation on Mac Hosts

For Mac OS X hosts, VirtualBox is available in a disk image (.dmg) file. The following steps will install VirtualBox on Mac OS X:

1. Double-click the disk image file to mount its contents.

2. Double-click the VirtualBox.mpkg installer file displayed in the window.

3. Select the location to install VirtualBox.

4. After installation, find the VirtualBox icon in the Applications folder in the Finder, and you can drag the icon to the Dock, as shown in Figure 5-19.

Figure 5-18 Create a new, empty VM for installing Windows Vista.

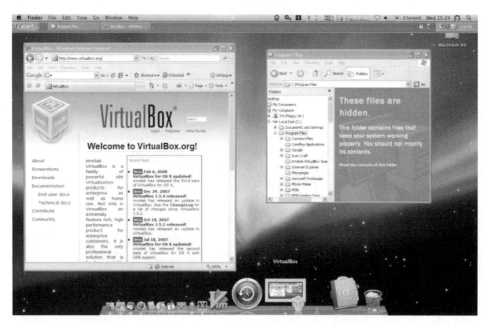

Figure 5-19   Users can drag the VirtualBox icon to the Dock after installation.

Sun Virtual Desktop Infrastructure Software

Sun Virtual Desktop Infrastructure (VDI) Software deploys a secure, resilient, and available desktop environment. VDI Software provides the following features:

- Provides secure access to virtual desktop environments
- Supports Sun Ray devices, traditional PCs, and the VMware back end
- Improved scalability with support for multiple VMware virtual center servers
- Simplified integration with Sun Secure Global Desktop Software
- Additional access to virtual desktops using RDP clients
- Enhanced storage mechanism for virtual machines using the ZFS file system
- Usage of MySQL as the configuration database

Figure 5-20 shows the VDI architecture.

Security Concerns with Sun Virtualization

Sun virtualization faces the following security concerns:

- Sun xVM Server enables network traffic encryption between guests to lessen the risk of attacks between guests on a node.
- Centralized access to all virtual machines leads to a critical security vulnerability point.
- By compromising the virtualization platform, an intruder can steal virtual machines and gain access to their data.

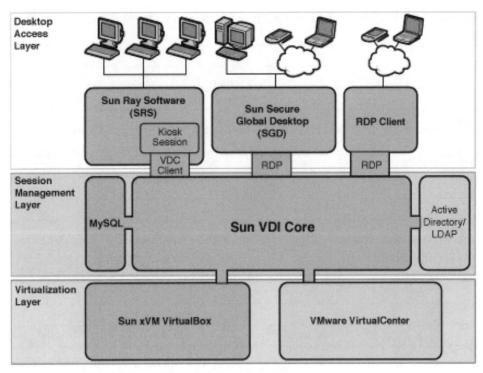

Figure 5-20 VDI architecture provides data isolation.

Chapter Summary

- Sun provides a range of open, scalable virtualization products and services.
- Sun virtualization products include Sun xVM Server, Sun xVM Ops Center, and Sun xVM VirtualBox.
- With the enterprise controller, users can manage connected systems using a user-friendly browser-based interface.
- VirtualBox is an x86 virtualization product.
- Sun Virtual Desktop Infrastructure Software deploys a secure, resilient, and available desktop environment.

Review Questions

1. Explain the uses of virtualization.

   _____

   _____

   _____

   _____

2. Discuss Sun desktop virtualization and its business and operational benefits.

   _____

   _____

   _____

   _____

3. Explain the Sun xVM Ops Center architecture for the connected and disconnected modes.

   _____

   _____

   _____

   _____

4. List the various steps involved in the installation of the Sun xVM Ops Center.

   _____

   _____

   _____

   _____

5. List the various steps involved in the installation and configuration of Sun xVM Ops Center Enterprise Controller software.

   _____

   _____

   _____

   _____

6. List the various steps involved in the installation and configuration of Sun xVM Ops Center Proxy Controller software.

   _____

   _____

   _____

   _____

7. Discuss the Sun xVM VirtualBox and its architecture.

   _____

   _____

   _____

   _____

8. List the various steps involved in the installation of VirtualBox on Windows hosts.

   _____

   _____

   _____

   _____

9. What are the security challenges to Sun virtualization products?

   _____

   _____

   _____

   _____

Hands-On Projects

1. Navigate to Chapter 5 of the Student Resource Center. Open grid_containers.pdf and read the following topics:

   - Server Virtualization
   - Containers At Work
   - The Evolution of Containers

2. Navigate to Chapter 5 of the Student Resource Center. Open virtual_sb.pdf and read the following topics:

   - Server Virtualization
   - Server and OS support for resource management
   - Virtual machine monitors

3. Navigate to Chapter 5 of the Student Resource Center. Open virtualization_lc (System Virtualization).pdf and read the following topics:

   - Situation Overview
   - Server Virtualization: The Need for Choice
   - Types of Server Virtualization

## Chapter 6

Red Hat Enterprise Linux Virtualization

Objectives

After completing this chapter, you should be able to:

- Implement Red Hat Virtualization
- Understand the requirements for Red Hat Virtualization
- Create a guest operating system
- Install Red Hat Enterprise Linux 5 as a paravirtualized guest
- Install Windows XP as a fully virtualized guest
- Create a virtualized floppy disk controller
- Add storage devices to guests

Key Terms

Full virtualization   a type of virtualization that does not require any modifications to guest operating systems

Introduction to Red Hat Enterprise Linux Virtualization

Red Hat Linux is one of the most popular lightweight, open-source platforms. The enterprise version of Red Hat Linux provides a multilayered virtualization system driven by the Red Hat Virtualization component. This chapter teaches you how to implement this virtualization system.

Red Hat Enterprise Linux Virtualization Basics

Red Hat Enterprise Linux can host multiple guest operating systems, with each guest operating system running in its own domain. It schedules the virtual CPUs within the virtual machines in order to make the best use of the available physical CPUs. Each guest operating system handles its own applications and schedules each application accordingly.

Red Hat Virtualization can be deployed in two ways: full virtualization and paravirtualization. *Full virtualization* creates a new virtual machine in which the guest operating systems can run. It does not require any modification to the guest operating system or application; the guest OS or application is not aware of the virtualized environment. Paravirtualization requires user modification of the guest operating systems that run on the virtual machines. These guest operating systems are aware that they are running on a virtual machine. Paravirtualization provides near-native levels of performance.

The first domain, known as Domain0, is automatically created when the user boots the system. Domain0 is an authorized guest that creates domains and manages virtual resources. It manages physical hardware and performs administrative tasks such as resuming, suspending, or shifting guest domains to other virtual machines.

Red Hat's Virtual Machine Monitor, called the hypervisor, is a virtualization platform that allows multiple operating systems to run on a single host simultaneously within a full virtualization environment. A guest is an OS that runs on a virtual machine in addition to the host or main OS.

The user can configure guest machines with a number of virtual CPUs (called VCPUs). The Virtual Machine Manager schedules the VCPUs according to the workload on the physical CPUs. The user can grant any number of virtual disks, as well as network and other interfaces, to the guest.

System Requirements

Running virtualization on Red Hat Enterprise Linux requires the following:

- Computer system running Red Hat Enterprise Linux 5 Server with virtualization packages
- Configured hypervisor host
- 6 GB of free disk space per guest
- 2 GB of RAM per guest
- 6 GB plus per guest
- One processing core or hyperthread for each guest and one for the hypervisor (recommended)

Paravirtualized guests require the Red Hat Enterprise Linux 5 installation tree be available over NFS, FTP, or HTTP. Fully virtualized guests require an installation disc, as well as CPUs with hardware virtualization extensions. To verify whether the virtualization extensions are enabled or disabled in the BIOS of an Intel-based machine, users can follow these steps:

1. Run the **xm dmesg | grep VMX** command. The output should display:

```
(XEN) VMXON is done
(XEN) VMXON is done
```

2. Run the **cat /proc/cpuinfo | grep vmx** command to verify that the CPU flags have been set. The output should display:

```
flags:fpu tsc msr pae mce cx8 apic mtrr mca cmov pat pse36 clflush
dts acpi mmx fxsr sse sse2 ss ht tm syscall lm constant _ tsc pni
monitor ds _ cpl vmx est tm2 cx16 xtpr lahf _ lm
```

Users can run the following commands to verify the virtualization extensions on systems with AMD-V architectures:

1. Run the **xm dmesg | grep SVM** command. The output should look like the following:

```
(XEN) AMD SVM Extension is enabled for cpu 0
(XEN) AMD SVM Extension is enabled for cpu 1
```

2. Run the **cat /proc/cpuinfo | grep svm** command to verify that the CPU flags have been set. The output should look like the following:

```
flags:fpu tsc msr pae mce cx8 apic mtrr mca cmov pat pse36 clflush mmx
fxsr sse sse2 ht syscall nx mmxext fxsr _ opt lm 3dnowext 3dnow pni cx16
lahf _ lm cmp _ legacy svm cr8legacy ts fid vid ttp tm stc
```

Supported guest storage methods include the following:

- Files on local storage
- Physical disk partitions
- Locally connected LUNs
- LVM partitions
- iSCSI and Fibre Channel–based LUNs

Installing Red Hat Enterprise Linux Virtualization

Users should perform the following steps prior to the Red Hat installation:

- Enable Red Hat Network (RHN) entitlements for the Red Hat Virtualization packages.
- Enable all entitlements to install and update the virtualization packages on Red Hat Enterprise Linux.
- Register the machines with RHN and create a valid Red Hat Network account for the installation process at http://rhn.redhat.com.

To add a virtualization element with RHN, users can follow these steps:

1. Enable RHN entitlements for the Red Hat Virtualization packages.
2. Enter the RHN username and password to log on to RHN.
3. Select the systems on which to install Red Hat Virtualization.
4. Check the **Virtualization** check box in the **System Properties** section where the system entitlements are listed.

After completing the above steps, the system should start receiving the Red Hat Virtualization packages.

Installing Using the yum Command

Installing Red Hat Virtualization on Red Hat Enterprise Linux requires the following packages:

- *xen*: This package contains the fundamental virtualization tools and the hypervisor.
- *kernel-xen*: This package contains the modified Linux kernel that works as a virtual machine guest on the hypervisor.

Users can follow these steps to install the xen and kernel-xen packages:

1. Type the following command:

   ```
   yum install xen kernel-xen
   ```

2. Fully virtualized guests on systems with Itanium architecture require the guest firmware image package (xen-ia64-guest-firmware) from the installation DVD. To install this package, run the following command:

   ```
   yum install xen-ia64-guest-firmware
   ```

3. To install other recommended virtualization packages, run the following command:

   ```
   yum install virt-manager libvirt libvirt-python libvirt-python
   python-virtinst
   ```

The following Linux virtualization packages are recommended:

- *python-virtinst*: This package provides the virt-install command for creating virtual machines.
- *libvirt*: This is an API library used to interact with hypervisors, as well as control and manage virtual machines.
- *libvirt-python*: This package allows applications written in the Python programming language to use the interface provided by the libvirt API.
- *virt-manager*: This package provides a graphical tool for creating and managing the virtualized guests.

Creating Guests with virt-manager

virt-manager (Virtual Machine Manager) is a package that provides a graphical tool for creating and managing virtualized guests. Users can perform the following steps to create guests with virt-manager:

1. Start virt-manager by typing the following command:

   ```
   sudo virt-manager &
   ```

2. Click the **Connect** button in the **Open connection** dialog box.

3. Click the **New** button in the **Virtual Machine Manager** window to create a new guest.

4. Read the information on the screen and click the **Forward** button.

5. In the **Choosing a virtualization method** window, select the virtualization type and then click the **Forward** button.

6. In the **Locating installation media** window, specify the installation media and then click the **Forward** button.

7. In the **Assigning storage space** window, select a disk partition, select a LUN, or create an image file for guest storage. The installation process automatically selects the size of the guest's swap file according to the amount of RAM allocated to the guest. Click the **Forward** button when finished.

8. In the **Allocate memory and CPU** window, choose the appropriate values for the virtualized CPUs and memory allocation and then click the **Forward** button.

9. The **Ready to begin installation** window presents a summary of all configuration information. Review the information and, if necessary, use the **Back** button to make changes. Otherwise, click the **Finish** button to begin the installation process.

Installing Guest Operating Systems

Various operating systems can be installed as guest operating systems in a virtualized environment on Red Hat Enterprise Linux. There are several types of guest operating system installation processes, including the following:

- Installing Red Hat Enterprise Linux 5 as a paravirtualized guest from a shell
- Installing Windows XP as a fully virtualized guest
- Creating a fully virtualized Windows Server 2003 SP1 guest

Installing Red Hat Enterprise Linux 5 as a Paravirtualized Guest

Paravirtualization is faster than full virtualization and has most of the same advantages. Paravirtualization requires the kernel-xen kernel. The paravirtualization installation process requires root privileges or sudo access.

Users can use the virt-manager or virt-install command to create paravirtualized Red Hat Enterprise Linux 5 guests. They can run the following command to open the Virtual Machine Console window:

```
virt-install -n rhel5PV -r 500 -fvar/lib/xen/images/rhel5PV.dsk -s 3
--vnc -p -l\ftp://10.1.1.1/trees/RHEL5-B2-Server-i386/
```

In this command the --vnc option specified a graphical installation, *rhel5PV* is the name of the guest, *rhel5PV.dsk* is the disk image, and *ftp://10.1.1.1/trees/RHEL5-B2-Server-i386/* is the local mirror of the Red Hat Enterprise Linux 5 installation tree.

After completing the initial boot phase, the standard installation process for Red Hat Enterprise Linux starts. Users can follow these steps to install Red Hat Enterprise Linux as the guest OS:

1. Select the proper language and select **OK**.

2. Select the keyboard layout and select **OK**.

3. Choose the TCP/IP options and select **OK**.

   - If DHCP is selected, the installation process attempts to obtain an IP address. Otherwise, manually enter the IP information and select **OK**.

4. The installation process now retrieves the files it needs from the server. Once the initial steps are complete, the graphical installation process starts. Click the **Next** button.

   • If installing a beta version of Red Hat Enterprise Linux 5, the warning shown in Figure 6-1 will appear. Click the **Install anyway** button, and then click the **Next** button.

5. Enter a valid registration code in the **Installation Number** field and click the **OK** button.

6. The installation process asks to confirm the deletion of all data on the storage device. Click the **Yes** button.

7. Review the storage configuration and partition layout. Click the **Advanced storage configuration** button to use iSCSI. Otherwise, click the **Next** button.

8. Click the **Yes** button to confirm that Linux partitions will be removed.

9. Configure networking and hostname settings and click the **Next** button.

10. Select the time zone for the environment and click the **Next** button.

11. Enter the root password for the guest and click the **Next** button.

12. Check the boxes corresponding to the software packages to install. Select the **Customize Now** radio button and click the **Next** button.

13. The installer will check software dependencies. Click the **Next** button.

14. Click the **Next** button once more to begin the installation process.

15. After the installation is finished, click **Reboot** to restart the guest.

16. Once the system reboots, open virt-manager. Select the name of the guest OS, click **Open**, and then click **Run**.

17. At the **Welcome** window, click the **Forward** button.

18. Read and accept the license agreement and click the **Forward** button.

19. Enable the firewall, check the boxes for the trusted services, and click the **Forward** button.

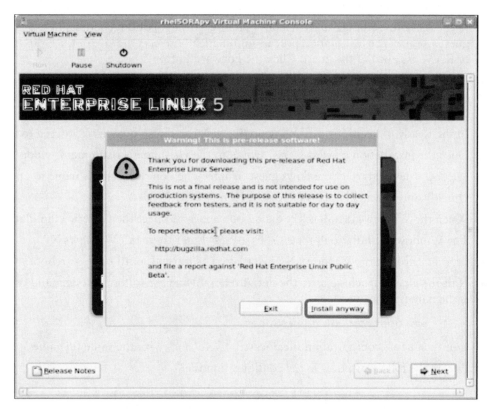

Figure 6-1   Click the **Install anyway** button if this warning appears.

20. Set SELinux to enforcing mode and click the **Forward** button.

21. If required, enable kdump and click the **Forward** button.

22. Set the date and time for the guest and click the **Forward** button. This date and time must match that of the hypervisor.

23. In the **Set up software updates** window, click the **Forward** button.

24. Confirm the choices for RHN and click the **Forward** button.

25. At the **Finish Update Setup** window, click the **Forward** button.

26. Create a nonroot user account and click the **Forward** button.

27. Set up the sound card, if required, and click the **Forward** button.

28. At the **Additional CDs** window, install any additional software packages from the CD and click the **Finish** button to complete the installation.

29. The Red Hat Enterprise Linux 5 login screen will appear. Log in using the username created in Step 26.

30. A window containing a paravirtualized Red Hat Enterprise Linux guest will appear.

Installing a Windows XP Guest

To install Windows XP as a fully virtualized guest, users can follow these steps:

1. Go to Applications, then System Tools, and then Virtual Machine Manager to open the virtual machine manager.

2. Click **File** and then **Open Connection** to open a connection to the host.

3. Click the **New** button to create a new virtual machine.

4. At the **Naming your virtual system** screen, enter the system name and click the **Forward** button.

5. At the **Choosing a virtualization method** window, select the fully virtualized option and click the **Forward** button.

6. On the **Locating installation media** window, specify the location of the Windows installation disc and click the **Forward** button.

7. In the **Assigning storage space** window, choose a disk partition, choose a LUN, or create an image file for guest storage. The installation process automatically selects the size of the swap file based on the amount of RAM assigned to the guest. Click the **Forward** button.

8. In the **Allocate memory and CPU** window, choose the appropriate values for the virtualized CPUs and memory allocation and click the **Forward** button. Do not allocate more virtual CPUs than physical processors (or hyperthreads) available on the host system.

9. In the **Ready to begin installation** window, click the **Finish** button to proceed to the OS installation.

10. Once the installation process starts, switch to the **virt-manager summary** window.

11. Select the newly started Windows guest. Double-click on the system's name to open the console window.

12. Quickly and repeatedly press F5 to select a new HAL.

13. When the **Windows install select** dialog box appears, select the **Generic i486 Platform** tab.

14. The Windows installation process starts. Press Enter to install Windows XP.

15. Proceed through the Windows XP installation as normal, until the first reboot.

16. Halt the virtual machine after the initial reboot using the following command, where <WindowsGuest> is the name of the guest:

```
xm destroy <WindowsGuest>
```

17. Edit the guest's configuration file, located in /etc/xen/, with the same filename as the guest's name.

18. Locate the following entry in the configuration file:

```
k = ['file:/var/lib/xen/images/winxp.dsk,hda,w']
```

Change this entry to the following:

```
disk = ['file:/var/lib/xen/images/winxp.dsk,hda,w', 'file:/xen/pub/trees/
MS/en_winxp_pro_with_sp2.iso,hdc:cdrom,r',]
```

19. Restart the Windows guest with the **xm create <WindowsGuest>** command.

20. Continue with the Windows XP installation as normal. If the installation freezes for an extended period of time, restart the guest operating system with the **virsh reboot <WindowsGuest>** command.

21. Once setup is finished the window should show a Windows desktop.

Configuring Red Hat Enterprise Linux Virtualization

Creating a Virtualized Floppy Disk Controller

Floppy disk controllers are needed for many older operating systems, particularly those that do not natively support CD or DVD controllers. A virtualized floppy disk controller must be created to access the floppy disk devices. This requires the image file of a floppy disk. Users can use the dd command to create a floppy disk image file as follows:

sudo dd if=/dev/fd0 of=~/legacydrivers.img

In the above example, /dev/fd0 can be replaced with the name of a floppy disk device. A virtualized floppy disk controller can be created by following these steps:

1. On a running guest operating system, create the XML configuration file for the guest image using the **virsh** command:

    virsh dumpxml rhel5FV > rhel5FV.xml

2. Create a floppy disk image for the guest using the following command:

    sudo dd if=/dev/zero of=/var/lib/xen/images/rhel5FV-floppy.img bs=512 count=2880

3. Add the following to the guest's configuration XML file:

    ```
    <disk type='file' device='floppy'>
    <source file='/var/lib/xen/images/rhel5FV-floppy.img'/>
    <target dev='fda'/>
    </disk>
    ```

4. Stop the guest by running the **virsh stop rhel5FV** command.

5. Restart the guest by using the XML configuration file as follows:

    virsh create rhel5FV.xml

Adding Storage Devices to Guests

After creating guests, storage devices must be added to each virtual guest machine. Supported storage devices and protocols include the following:

- Local hard drive partitions
- Logical volumes
- Fibre Channel or iSCSI directly connected to the host
- File containers residing in a file system on the host
- NFS file systems mounted directly by the virtual machine
- iSCSI storage directly accessed by the guest
- Clustered file systems

Users can perform the following steps to add file-based storage to a guest OS:

1. Create an empty container file using the dd command. Create a sparse file by using the following command:

   ```
   sudo dd if=/dev/zero of=/xen/images/FileName.img bs=1M seek=4096
   count=0
   ```

   Alternatively, create a nonsparse file using the following command:

   ```
   sudo dd if=/dev/zero of=/xen/images/FileName.img bs=1M count=4096
   ```

2. Dump the configuration for the guest:

   ```
   sudo virsh dumpxml Guest1 > ~/Guest1.xml
   ```

3. Open the configuration file in a text editor, as shown in Figure 6-2.

4. Add additional storage by modifying the *end of disk=* entry, as shown in Figure 6-3.

5. Restart the guest operating system from the updated configuration file:

   ```
   sudo virsh create Guest1.xml
   ```

6. The guest operating system now uses the file FileName.img as the device called /dev/hdb. On the guest operating system, partition the device into one primary partition for the complete device and format the device as follows:

   - Run the following command and then press n for a new partition:

     ```
     fdisk /dev/hdb
     ```

   - Press p for a primary partition and choose an available partition number.

     Partition number (1–4): **1**

   - Enter the default first cylinder by pressing Enter.

     First cylinder (1–400, default 1):

   - Select the size of the partition.

     Last cylinder or +size or +sizeM or +sizeK (2–400, default 400):

```
>disk type='file' device='disk'<
        >driver name='tap' type='aio'/<
        >source file='/var/lib/libvirt/images/Guest1.img'/<
        >target dev='xvda'/<
>/disk<
```

Figure 6-2   Open the configuration file in a text editor.

```
>disk type='file' device='disk'<
        >driver name='tap' type='aio'/<
        >source file='/var/lib/libvirt/images/Guest1.img'/<
        >target dev='xvda'/<
>/disk<
>disk type='file' device='disk'<
        >driver name='tap' type='aio'/<
        >source file='/xen/images/FileName.img'/<
        >target dev='hda'/<
>/disk<
```

Figure 6-3   Modify the *end of disk=* entry to add additional storage.

- Set the type of partition by pressing t.

    Command (m for help): **t**

- Choose the partition created in the previous steps.

    Partition number (1–4): **1**

- Enter 83 for a Linux partition.

    Hex code (type L to list codes): **83**

- Write the changes to disk and quit.

    Command (m for help): **w**

    Command (m for help): **q**

- Format the new partition with the ext3 file system

    ```
    mke2fs -j /dev/hdb
    ```

7. Mount the disk on the guest OS.

    ```
    mount /dev/hdb1 /myfiles
    ```

Adding a Virtualized CD-ROM or DVD Device to a Guest

To attach an ISO file to a guest when the guest is online, users can use the virsh command with the attach-disk parameter as follows:

```
virsh attach-disk [domain-id] [source] [target] --driver file –type
cdrom --mode readonly
```

In the above example, *[source]* represents the path for the files and devices on the host, and *[target]* represents the path for the files and devices on the guest.

Configuring Networks and Guests

Configuring networks and guests in Red Hat Virtualization involves installing multiple Ethernet interfaces and setting up bridging. Every domain network interface is directly connected by a point-to-point link to a virtual network interface.

Red Hat Virtualization's virtual networking is controlled by two shell scripts: network-bridge and vif-bridge. xend calls these scripts when certain events occur. Queries are directly passed to the scripts to provide extra information. These scripts are located in the /etc/xen/scripts directory. The user can modify script properties by changing the xend-config.sxp configuration file in the /etc/xen directory.

- **network-bridge**
  - Use the network-bridge command when xend starts or stops.
  - This command generates the bridge xenbr0 and moves eth0 onto that bridge, changing the routing accordingly.
  - When xend finally exits, it deletes the bridge and removes eth0, restoring the original IP and routing configuration.
- **vif-bridge**
  - This is a script invoked for each virtual interface on the domain.
  - It configures firewall rules and configures a virtual interface in bridged mode.

Configuring Multiple Guest Network Bridges to Use Multiple Ethernet Cards

To set up multiple Red Hat Virtualization bridges, users can follow these steps:

1. By using the system-config-network application, configure another network interface. Create a new configuration file named ifcfg-eth1 in the /etc/sysconfig/network-scripts/ directory, as shown in Figure 6-4.

2. Copy the file /etc/xen/scripts/network-bridge to /etc/xen/scripts/networkbridge.xen.

3. Comment out any existing network scripts in /etc/xen/xend-config.sxp and add the following line:

    `network-xen-multi-bridge`

4. Create a custom script to create multiple Red Hat Virtualization network bridges, as shown in Figure 6-5.

Laptop Network Configuration

Users can perform the following steps to configure a laptop network on host/Dom0:

1. Create a dummy0 network interface and allocate a static IP address to it.

```
$ cat /etc/sysconfig/network-scripts/ifcfg-eth1
DEVICE=eth1
BOOTPROTO=static
ONBOOT=yes
USERCTL=no
IPV6INIT=no
PEERDNS=yes
TYPE=Ethernet
NETMASK=255.255.255.0
IPADDR=10.1.1.1
GATEWAY=10.1.1.254
ARP=yes
```

Figure 6-4   Create a new configuration file with these contents.

```
#!/bin/sh
# network-xen-multi-bridge
# Exit if anything goes wrong.
set -e
# First arg is the operation.
OP=$1
shift
script=/etc/xen/scripts/network-bridge.xen
case ${OP} in
start)
        $script start vifnum=1 bridge=xenbr1 netdev=eth1
        $script start vifnum=0 bridge=xenbr0 netdev=eth0
        ;;
stop)
        $script stop vifnum=1 bridge=xenbr1 netdev=eth1
        $script stop vifnum=0 bridge=xenbr0 netdev=eth0
        ;;
status)
        $script status vifnum=1 bridge=xenbr1 netdev=eth1
        $script status vifnum=0 bridge=xenbr0 netdev=eth0
        ;;
*)
        echo 'Unknown command: ' ${OP}
        echo 'Valid commands are: start, stop, status'
        exit 1
esac
```

Figure 6-5   Create a custom script like this one to create multiple
network bridges.

2. To enable dummy device support, add the following lines to /etc/modprobe.conf:

```
alias dummy0 dummy
options dummy numdummies=1
```

3. To configure networking for dummy0, edit the /etc/sysconfig/networkscripts/ifcfg-dummy0 file as shown in Figure 6-6.

4. Bind xenbr0 to dummy0 in order to use networking even when not connected to a physical network.

5. Edit /etc/xen/xend-config.sxp to include the *netdev=dummy0* entry as follows:

```
(network-script `network-bridge bridge=xenbr0 netdev=dummy0')
```

6. Open /etc/sysconfig/network in the guest OS and modify the default gateway to point to dummy0, as shown in Figure 6-7.

7. Set up network address translation (NAT) in the host to allow the guest to access the Internet, including wireless networks. NAT permits multiple network addresses to connect through a single IP address by intercepting packets and passing them to the private IP address. To configure NAT in Red Hat Virtualization, copy the script in Figure 6-8 to /etc/init.d/xenLaptopNAT and create a soft link to /etc/rc3.d/S99xenLaptopNAT.

```
DEVICE=dummy0
BOOTPROTO=none
ONBOOT=yes
USERCTL=no
IPV6INIT=no
PEERDNS=yes
TYPE=Ethernet
NETMASK=255.255.255.0
IPADDR=10.1.1.1
ARP=yes
```

Figure 6-6 Edit the /etc/sysconfig/networkscripts/ifcfg-dummy0 file like this.

```
NETWORKING=yes
HOSTNAME=localhost.localdomain
GATEWAY=10.1.1.1
IPADDR=10.1.1.10
NETMASK=255.255.255.0
```

Figure 6-7 Modify /etc/sysconfig/network in the guest OS like this.

```
#!/bin/bash
PATH=/usr/bin:/sbin:/bin:/usr/sbin
export PATH
GATEWAYDEV=`ip route | grep default | awk {'print $5'}`
iptables -F
case "$1" in
start)
        if test -z "$GATEWAYDEV"; then
        echo "No gateway device found"
    else
        echo  "Masquerading using $GATEWAYDEV"
        /sbin/iptables -t nat -A POSTROUTING -o $GATEWAYDEV -j MASQUERADE
fi
        echo "Enabling IP forwarding"
        echo 1 > /proc/sys/net/ipv4/ip_forward
        echo "IP forwarding set to `cat /proc/sys/net/ipv4/ip_forward`"
        echo "done."
        ;;
*)
echo "Usage: $0 {start|restart|status}"
;;
esac
```

Figure 6-8 Copy this script into /etc/init.d/xenLaptopNAT to configure NAT.

Chapter Summary

- To use Red Hat Virtualization, users require a system running Red Hat Enterprise Linux 5 Server with its virtualization packages.
- The Red Hat Virtualization system installation process involves installing a guest operating system in the virtualized environment and then configuring the Red Hat Virtualization system.

Review Questions

1. What is Red Hat Virtualization?

2. What is the difference between full virtualization and paravirtualization?

3. What are the basic system requirements for Red Hat Enterprise Linux Virtualization?

4. How does a user create guests with virt-manager?

5. Why is it necessary to create a virtualized floppy disk controller?

Hands-On Projects

1. Read about Linux virtualization.

   ■ Navigate to Chapter 6 of the Student Resource Center.
   ■ Open 3490182 (Linux Virtualization).pdf and read the content.

2. Read about virtualization tools.

   ■ Navigate to Chapter 6 of the Student Resource Center.
   ■ Open RHEL_5p3_wp_0109_web.pdf and read the content.

3. Read more about Linux virtualization.

   ■ Navigate to Chapter 6 of the Student Resource Center.
   ■ Open Virtualization.pdf and read the content.

## Chapter 7

NoMachine

Objectives

After completing this chapter, you should be able to:

- Explain how NX components work
- Describe the NX system architecture
- Install NX Client
- Configure the NX client
- Set up NX client sessions
- Install NX Node
- Install NX Server

Key Terms

NoMachine a network computing company established to provide remote access and terminal services for enterprises in migration to the Linux platform

NX technology a technology that compresses X-protocol traffic using differential compression and uses a proxy X server to reduce X-protocol roundtrips across the network

X client a general program that requires a graphical interface for interaction

X server a special program that draws the graphical interface of the X client and of any other running program onto the screen

X11 (or X) protocol a protocol used to build a basic desktop environment

Introduction to NoMachine

NoMachine is a network computing company established to provide remote access and terminal services for enterprises in migration to the Linux platform. NoMachine NX is an enterprise-class solution designed for the following purposes:

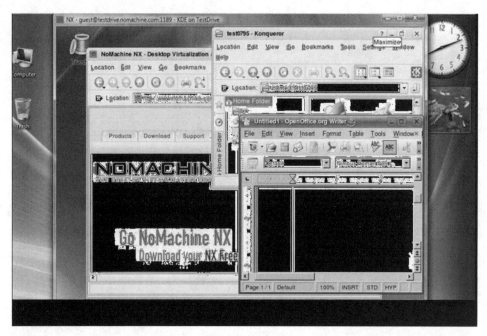

Figure 7-1 NoMachine NX allows the user to run virtualized desktops on a variety of platforms.

- Secure remote access
- Desktop virtualization
- Hosted desktop deployment

The NX server uses the *X11 (or X) protocol*. This protocol and the X Window System are used to build a basic desktop environment. NX does not require high-bandwidth network sessions to run remote X11 sessions. It is a platform-independent solution that can allow sessions to be executed from any client machines running on Windows, Linux, Mac OS X, and Solaris platforms to servers running on Linux or Solaris, as shown in Figure 7-1.

NX includes X protocol compression techniques and an integrated set of proxy agents to accomplish the following goals:

- Improve the power of the X Window System to transparently run graphical desktops and applications through the network
- Reduce roundtrips and implementation of the strict flow control of data traveling through low-bandwidth links
- Reduce the time required to start up any application
- Provide high performance even if the user is connected to a low-bandwidth network connection; NX's encoding algorithm automatically tunes itself to the network bandwidth and latency parameters

NX Server

NX Technology

NX technology compresses X-protocol traffic using differential compression. It uses a proxy X server to reduce X-protocol roundtrips across the network, as shown in Figure 7-2.

The X protocol is the basis for communication between the X server and the X client. The *X client* is a general program that requires a graphical interface for interaction; the *X server* is a special program that draws the graphical interface of the X client and any other running program onto the screen. The X client sends the requests to the X server, which in turn sends the responses, events, and errors (if any) to the X client.

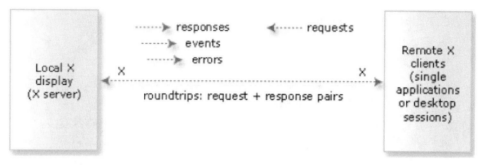

Figure 7-2 NX technology uses a proxy X server to reduce X-protocol roundtrips.

X Window System

NX distributed computing uses the X Window System for the following reasons:

- Makes network computing easy
- Provides widespread Web browsing
- Enables any UNIX computer to work as a terminal server and clients
- Supports a wide range of platforms and operating systems
- Windowing system offers graphical user interfaces for the Linux and UNIX operating systems

NX Performance

Using the NX method to run an X client and X server on different host machines provides the following advantages:

- An efficient compression of the X traffic
- Reduction in time-consuming X roundtrips
- The lazy encoding algorithm to defer screen updates

To see the difference NX makes, the user can play with its various configurations via the NX Client GUI (Figure 7-3).

NX Components at Work

The NX Server is composed of various components that can be installed in different configurations. Communication between the local and remote computers can be achieved by connecting a two-way proxy to the system. Proxies provided by the NX Client package communicate using the NX protocol, which is based on X11 sessions, as shown in Figure 7-4. These extensions are implemented to compress, cache, and reduce the roundtrip X traffic between the NX proxies to near zero. In this architecture, one proxy is on the local computer and the other system resides on the NX Server.

The local proxy (NX Client) communicates with the local X server, which helps translate the NX protocol back to X11. The remote proxy communicates with the remote X11 applications and uses the X11 protocol. The remote NX proxy acts as if it is the X server where all the roundtrips take place. However, because this happens on the same host machine, the roundtrips are quickly resolved using UNIX domain sockets. Both the local and remote proxies keep their own cache of transferred data. These two sets of caches are synchronized in order to prevent further transmission.

NX Sessions

NX sessions can be run in the following configurations:

- RDP and VNC sessions
  - NX supports either RDP or VNC sessions by running the RDP (rdesktop) or VNC (tightVNC) client directly within the X11 session.
  - NX may suspend or reconnect the session types and hence can access these sessions with the help of session shadowing.

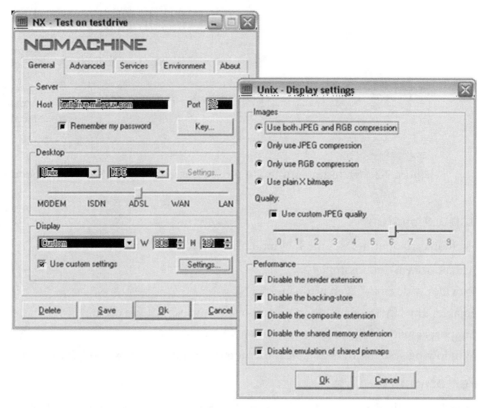

Figure 7-3 NX settings allow the user to configure the GUI in a number of different ways.

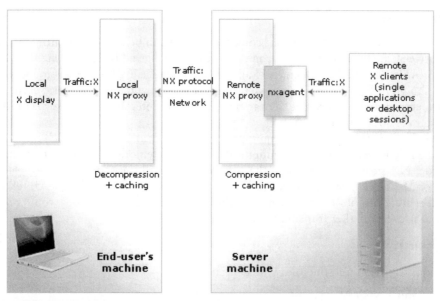

Figure 7-4 Proxies provided by the NX Client package communicate using the NX protocol, which is based on X11 sessions.

- Full desktop sessions
  - NX allows the user to run full desktop sessions, which can be displayed full screen on the local machine or in windowed mode.
  - The user can change the display size for the session window.
  - Desktop types such as KDE, GNOME, CDE, and XDM are supported.
- Single applications running in floating window mode
  - Single application window mode displays a floating window that draws a single remote application on the local screen.
  - In order to set up a single application, users select the custom desktop type in the NX Client GUI and specify the application.
- Session persistence
  - NX allows the user to disconnect a session, either a desktop or a floating-window session, from the remote display.
  - In this instance, the proxy agent will not be connected to any X client, and the user will be able to reconnect the session later.
- Desktop sharing and session shadowing
  - Desktop sharing and session shadowing are features that make NX suitable for a full range of different usage scenarios, such as remote help-desk activity and collaborative brainstorming.
  - NX offers the possibility of connecting to a local desktop (shadowing).
  - The server provides the list of available sessions to the client only upon the request of the end user.
- Printing support and file sharing
  - NX supports both SMBFS and CIFS protocols.
  - NX Client specifies to the server the operating system that is running when the session is configured to enable printer and file sharing.
  - The default protocol for printing and file sharing is CIFS for Windows NT–based, Linux, Mac OS X, and Solaris operating systems.

NX System Architecture

NoMachine offers software that helps customers access remote computers even if the systems are connected to slow or low-bandwidth Internet connections. It compresses the X protocol 50 times and makes the graphical applications usable over the Internet at a speed of 9.6 kbps. Figure 7-5 depicts the NX system architecture.

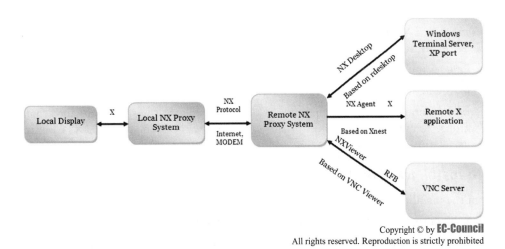

Figure 7-5 The NX system architecture compresses the X protocol 50 times.

NX Distributed Computing Architecture

NX distributed computing architecture is designed to distribute the workload between nodes in a wide area network (WAN). The NX Servers are intended to perform high-level manageability functions on the NX network. The distributed architecture ensures that nodes export their familiar computing environment to users' sessions run on NX node computers in a virtual cluster. Numerous NX nodes can be connected to one or more controlling servers to support thousands of concurrent sessions.

NX Installation and Configuration

Prerequisites

NX Server installation has the following prerequisites:

- Installation of the NX Client package
- Installation of the NX Node package

The following platforms support NX Client:

- Windows: 2000/2003/XP/Vista
- Mac OS X i386: 10.3/10.4
- Solaris SPARC: 8/9/10
- Mac OS X PPC: 10.3/10.4
- Linux i386:
  - Linux i386
  - Red Hat Enterprise Linux 4/5
  - SuSe 10/10.1/10.2/Enterprise 10
  - Mandriva 10.1/2005/2006/2007
  - Fedora Core 3/4/5/6
  - Fedora 7
  - Debian GNU/Linux 4.0 Etch
  - Ubuntu 5.10 Breezy Badger/6.06 Dapper Drake/6.10 Edgy Eft/7.04 Feisty Fawn
  - Xandros Desktop 4.1/Xandros Server 2.0

NX Server Tools

The following tools are components of the NX Server:

- *Nxagent*: Implements encapsulation and protocol translation of X
- *Nxsensor and Nxstat*: Daemons used by the NX Server Manager, the graphical administration interface of NX Server, to retrieve and display NX statistics
- *Nxclient*: A multifunctional GUI manager
- *Nxssh*: SSH client used to log in to the remote NX Server
- *Nxauth*: A command-line tool based on xauth that replaces the standard xauth that comes with X distributions. Nxauth handles X authorization cookies without the need for X11 libraries, saving space in the installation packages.

Steps to Install NX Client

1. Run the installation program.
2. Click **Next** to continue the installation process (Figure 7-6).
3. Select the destination to install NX Client by clicking the **Browse** option.
4. Click **Next** to proceed.
5. Select the Start Menu folder. Browse for the location and click **Next** (Figure 7-7).

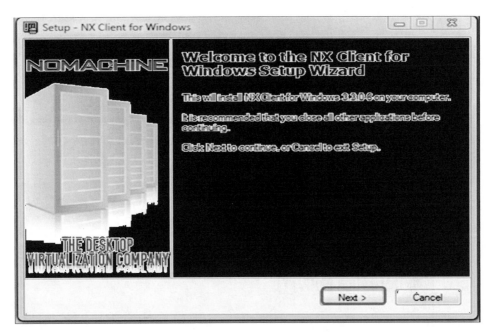

Figure 7-6   Click **Next** to continue the installation process.

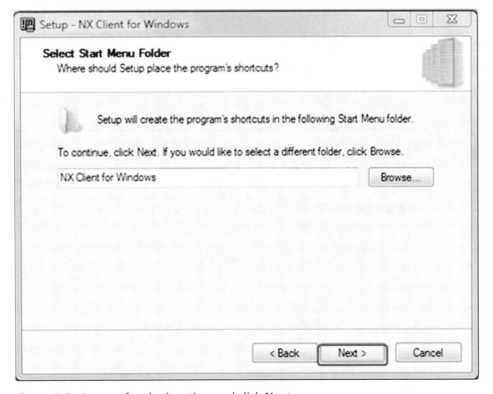

Figure 7-7   Browse for the location and click **Next**.

6. The **Select Additional Tasks** dialog box appears. Check the **Create a desktop icon** check box to create a desktop icon. Click **Next**.

7. The **Ready to Install** dialog box appears. Click **Install** to continue the installation process.

8. A dialog box saying "Completing the NX Client for Windows Setup Wizard" appears. Click **Finish** to exit setup (Figure 7-8).

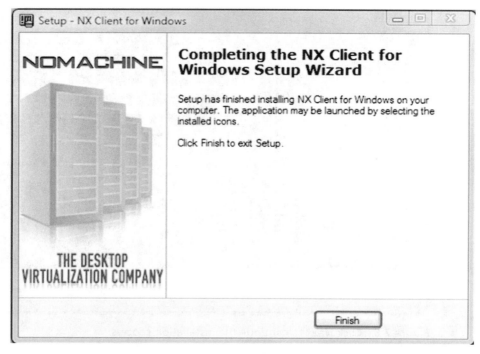

Figure 7-8   Click **Finish** to exit setup.

Steps to Configure NX Client

The following steps will configure the NX Client:

1. Open the NX Client Connection Wizard and click **Next** to start the configuration (Figure 7-9).

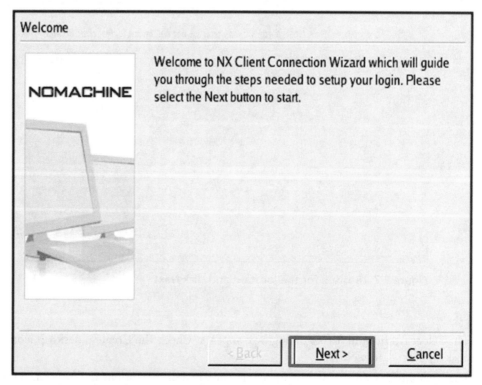

Figure 7-9   Click **Next** to start the configuration.

2. Provide the session name, hostname, and port number, and select the type of Internet connection (Figure 7-10). Click **Next** to continue.

3. Select the **operating system** and change settings, if any.

4. Select the command to run (/usr/bin/icewm), check **New virtual desktop**, and save the settings with the **OK** button (Figure 7-11).

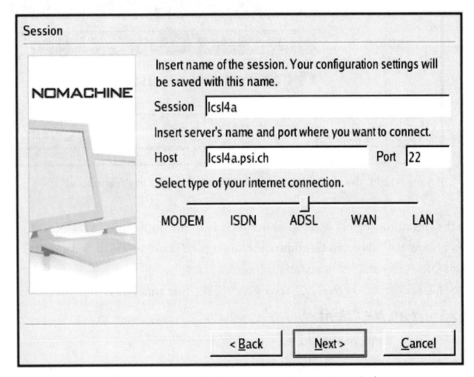

Figure 7-10   Provide the required information in the session window.

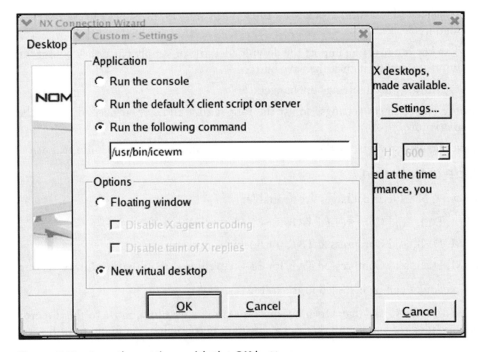

Figure 7-11   Save the settings with the **OK** button.

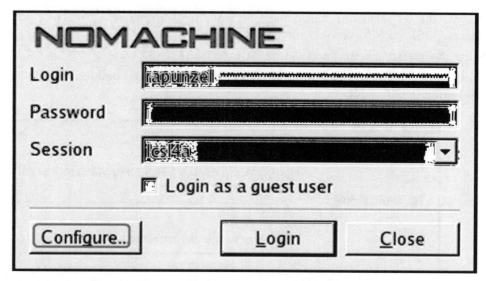

Figure 7-12   Enter the **login and session names** in the login window.

5. Set the size of the remote desktop to fit properly in the display, and click **Next** to proceed.
6. Select **Show the Advanced Configuration dialog** and click the **Finish** button.
7. Click **OK** to save the session configuration.
8. If SSH is being used on the NX Server host for the first time, then confirm the connection.

Steps to Start an NX Client

The following steps should be used to start an NX Client:

1. In the login window, type the login name and session name, and click **Configure** to continue (Figure 7-12).
2. In the **General configuration** tab, customize the desktop by selecting **Unix** and **Custom**, and clicking the **Settings** button (Figure 7-13).
3. Check the server key in case there are problems with the NX authentication.
   - If the key file client.id_dsa.key for the PSI NX servers (LCSL4a, LLCSL5A, etc.) is missing, then download it.
   - The key is a text file; import the downloaded file or simply paste the content into the **Key management** window, and then click the **Save** button.
4. Leave the advanced settings unchanged.
5. In the environment settings, adjust the font family and size, if needed, using the buttons in **Select NX fonts** (Figure 7-14).
6. Save the new settings for the specified session by clicking the **Save** and **OK** buttons.

NX Node Installation

The following NX Node packages are available:

- RPM, DEB, and Compressed TAR for 32-bit architecture
- RPM, DEB, and Compressed TAR for 64-bit architecture
- RPM, DEB, and Compressed TAR for 32-bit architecture for earlier Linux versions

These packages can be installed in the following ways:

- *NX Node RPM package*: Open an xterm or similar terminal, move to the directory the package was downloaded to, and install the package using the following command to utilize the rpm utility:

```
sudo rpm -ivh nxnode-X.Y.Z-W.i386.rpm
```

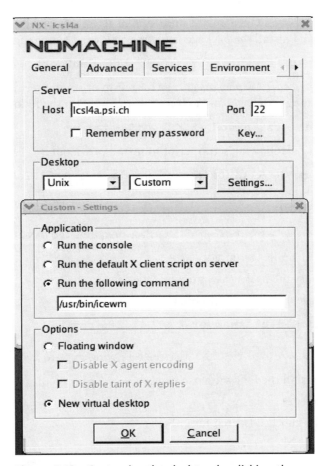

Figure 7-13   Customize the desktop by clicking the **Settings** button.

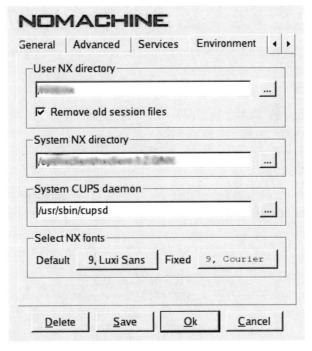

Figure 7-14   Customize the fonts in the environment settings.

- *NX Node DEB package*: Open an xterm or similar terminal, move to the directory the package was downloaded to, and install the package using the following command to utilize the dpkg utility:

  sudo dpkg -i nxnode _ X.Y.Z-W _ i386.debPackage

- *NX Node Compressed TAR package*: Open an xterm or similar terminal, go to the directory containing the downloaded tar.gz package, and extract the archive with the following command:

  sudo tar xvzf nxnode-X.Y.Z-W.i386.tar.gz

Then, users can run the following setup script to install NX Node:

sudo /usr/NX/scripts/setup/nxnode --installPlatforms

NX Server Installation

Installing the NX Server RPM Package Steps for installing the NX Server RPM Package are as follows:

1. Open an xterm or similar terminal.
2. Go to the directory the package was downloaded to.
3. Install the package using the RPM utility:

   sudo rpm -ivh nxserver-X.Y.Z-W.i386.rpm

Steps to Install NX Server on Debian Use the following steps to install NX Server on Debian:

1. Search for and install the following packages:
   - OpenSSH server
   - libstdc++2.10-glibc2.2 (search for glibc)
2. Install and run the NX Server.
   - Download the packages in Figure 7-15 from the NoMachine Web site using wget.
   - Install the packages in the following order:
     1. NX Client
     2. NX Node
     3. NX Server
   - Start the SSH server and NX Server using the commands in Figure 7-16.

```
wget http://64.34.161.181/download/2.1.0/Linux-
NoXft/nxclient_2.1.0-17_i386.deb
wget http://64.34.161.181/download/2.1.0/Linux/nxnode_2.1.0-22_i386.deb
wget http://64.34.161.181/download/2.1.0/Linux/FE/nxserver_2.1.0-22_i386.deb
```

Figure 7-15   Download the necessary packages using wget.

```
/etc/init.d/ssh start
/etc/init.d/nxserver start
```

Figure 7-16   Start the SSH
server and NX Server using
these commands.

Chapter Summary

- NoMachine NX is an enterprise-class solution for secure remote access, desktop virtualization, and hosted desktop deployment.
- NoMachine NX's distributed computing architecture is built on the foundations of the X Window System.
- NX technology compresses X-protocol traffic using differential compressions that reduce the number of X-protocol roundtrips across the network by using a proxy X server.
- NX's use of X compression techniques provides high performance even if the user is connected to low-bandwidth network connections.

Review Questions

1. What is NoMachine NX?

2. Explain NX technology.

3. Discuss different NX components.

4. Explain how NX sessions work.

5. Discuss the NX system architecture.

6. Discuss the NX distributed computing architecture.

7. List the various steps involved in the installation of NX Client.

_____

_____

_____

_____

8. List the various steps needed to configure NX Client.

_____

_____

_____

_____

9. List the steps to start NX Client.

_____

_____

_____

_____

10. List the steps to install NX Server on Debian.

_____

_____

_____

_____

Hands-On Projects

1. Navigate to Chapter 7 of the Student Resource Center. Open intr-components.pdf and read the following topics:

   ▪ Introduction to NX Software Components

   ▪ NX Libraries Installation Directory

   ▪ The User NX Directory

2. Navigate to Chapter 7 of the Student Resource Center. Open intr-technology (Introduction to NX technology).pdf and read the following topics:

   ▪ Introduction to NX Technology

   ▪ NoMachine's X Protocol Compression Technology

   ▪ NX Distributed Computing Architecture

3. Navigate to Chapter 7 of the Student Resource Center. Open admin-guide.pdf and read the following topics:

   ▪ Installing the NX Server

   ▪ An Overview of the Backend

   ▪ Services Management

Virtualization Security

Objectives

After completing this chapter, you should be able to:

- Understand the importance of virtualization security
- Recognize common attacks on virtual machines
- Understand the top virtualization security concerns
- Secure a virtual server environment

Key Terms

Golden image a disk image of a virtual machine's hard drive

Introduction to Virtualization Security

Virtualization is an emerging technology, making it of great concern to security professionals. Some security considerations include data leakage, improper authorization and access, and corruption of information assets. It is difficult to monitor the interactions between virtual machines on the same host, making forensics more difficult. Perhaps worst of all, if the hypervisor is compromised in any way, all of its virtual machines are compromised as well. This chapter teaches you how to ensure the confidentiality, integrity, and accessibility of virtualized environments.

Virtualization Security Benefits

Virtualized environments provide the following security benefits:

- *Isolation*: Virtual machines (VMs) can be configured as isolated and independent environments. If a system gets infected, it is less likely to affect other VMs.

- *Abstraction*: An abstraction layer between the VM and the underlying physical hardware limits potential damage. Physical hard disks remain undamaged even if the entire virtual hard disk is corrupted.
- *Deployment*: Workloads can be split across multiple systems using virtualization technology. A Web server component can gain secure access using HTTPS.
- *Portability*: The process of moving or copying workloads is simplified because VMs are hardware independent. If a security breach is detected, a VM can be shut down on one host system and booted on another system.
- *Rollback*: A VM can be rolled back to a particular point in time if a security violation occurs.

Virtualization Issues

The following are some issues that may arise at the various stages of a virtualization project:

- Analysis and planning
  - Compatibility and support
  - Licensing
  - Planning (migrating physical servers, installing consolidated virtual servers, and determining the number of virtual machines per physical server)
  - Staff training
  - Evaluating ROI (return on investment)
- Adaptation and postadaptation period
  - Reliability (poor backup practices or hardware failure)
  - Deployment
  - Evaluating efficiency
- Maintenance
  - Uneven scalability
  - Security
  - Unclear responsibilities
  - Evaluation of the virtualization market to ensure the best solution is used

Organizations must keep the following issues in mind at all stages:

- If the host is compromised, it is possible to take down the client servers hosted on the primary host machine.
- If the virtual network is compromised, the client is also compromised.
- Client shares and host shares need to be secured.
- A problem with the host machine can cause all VMs to terminate.
- VM security is as important as the security of single systems. Do not forget the principle of least privilege, which states that a user should be given the least amount of access to the system required to complete his or her job.
- Individual virtualization features, such as clipboard sharing, drag-and-drop support, file sharing between the host and guest, and APIs for programmatic access, may compromise the security of the complete virtual infrastructure if they have any bugs.
- Virtual disks are generally stored as unencrypted files on the host. An attacker who gains access to these files will gain the same level of access as a legitimate user.
- Virtualization adds new channels of network traffic, which could come under attack.
- It is harder to patch bare-metal hypervisors if a vulnerability is discovered, due to the increased complexity associated with flashing firmware-based components.

Common Attacks on Virtual Machines

The following are some of the attacks commonly launched against virtual machines:

- *Denial of service (DoS)*: A DoS attack can shut down a hypervisor. Using this attack, an attacker can plant a backdoor to access underlying VMs.
- *Virtual machine jumping*: If there is a security hole in the hypervisor, a user logged into one VM can jump to another VM.
- *Host traffic interception*: By exploiting a vulnerability in the hypervisor, an attacker can track system calls, paging files, memory, and disk activity.

Top Virtualization Security Concerns

The following are some of the most pressing virtualization security concerns:

- *Managing oversight and responsibility*: Organizations should employ a centralized system administrator or administrators to manage and guard all virtualized assets.
- *Patching and maintenance*: System administrators must install patches regularly. They should regularly store disk images of VM hard drives, sometimes called **golden images**, in order to quickly recover from a disaster.
- *VM sprawl*: Administrators should make sure that there are not more VMs than are necessary. They should keep track of all running VMs in order to avoid wasting resources and providing additional entry points for a potential attack.
- *Managing virtual appliances*: Many operating systems and applications include virtual appliances, which must be managed properly. The easiest way to do so is to buy virtual infrastructures from third-party vendors.
- *Visibility and compliance*: Virtual servers are almost invisible to data center managers who do not monitor all of the interactions between VMs inside a host. To visualize this activity, it becomes necessary to install virtualized security controls such as virtual firewalls and virtual sniffers.

Virtualization Security Considerations

Organizations must keep the following facts in mind when implementing and using virtualization:

- *Virtualization involves adding an operating system*: Virtual servers operate as real servers running operating systems such as Windows and Linux. Installing different operating systems on a single platform is difficult and may lead to a security risk.
- *Malware can spread among virtual servers*: Viruses and other malware can spread easily from one virtual server to another, because many intrusion detection systems do not detect activity between virtual servers on the same host. Many malware authors know this and create their malicious software specifically to exploit these vulnerabilities. Virtual firewalls can protect virtual servers.
- *Confidential data can be compromised*: Because the traffic flow between the virtual servers that share the same physical server cannot be adequately monitored, there is no way to ensure that confidential data have not been compromised. These data should be isolated on a separate physical server.
- *Outsourcers may not know any of the above*: When using hosted servers or outsourcing IT security, organizations must ensure that the provider is conscious of these security issues and has suitable protections. These extra protections should be part of the outsourcing agreement.

Virtualization Costs

Many companies consolidate a data center's physical servers into a virtual environment in order to gain increased operational efficiency and higher server utilization. A server running many VMs has a higher utilization rate than a server running on its own. A physical server hosting many virtual machines is in use about 80% of the time it is powered on, while nonvirtualized servers are typically in use about 15% of the time they are powered on. This leads to more efficient power utilization, as shown in Figure 8-1.

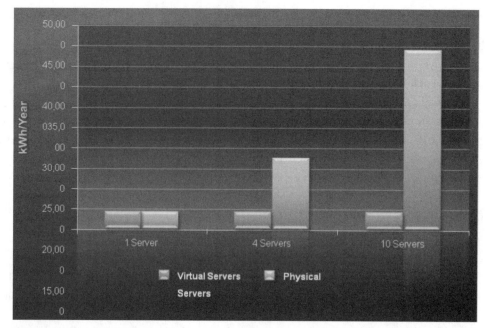

Figure 8-1 As the number of virtual servers increases, the total power utilization does not, making virtualized environments much more energy efficient.

Virtualization Security Checklist

Administrators should follow this checklist to secure a virtual server environment:

- Carefully consider virtualization products before committing.
- Keep the operating systems, host drivers, and applications on all VMs and the host updated.
- Install only what is required on the host and VMs.
- Use IPSec or strong encryption between the host and the VM.
- Do not browse the Web from the host computer.
- Secure the administrator accounts on the host computer.
- Turn off unused VMs.
- VMs must be incorporated into the enterprise security policy.
- Unused hardware ports on the VM, such as USB, should be disabled.
- The sharing of hardware resources should be limited.
- Avoid the sharing of IP addresses.
- Server administrators should have a defined plan for planning, deploying, and patching virtual machines.
- Back up the VMs regularly.

Chapter Summary

- Some of the security considerations involved with virtualization are data leakage, improper authorization and access, and corruption of information assets.

- A large number of companies are deploying virtualization technologies to increase operational efficiency, gain higher server utilization, and attain more efficient power utilization.

- Virtualization technology brings new risks.

Review Questions

1. What are some uses for virtualization?

2. What are some features and security benefits of virtualization?

3. What are some problems at the various stages of virtualization projects?

4. What are some common attacks on virtual machines?

5. What are the security risks of virtualization?

6. What are some actions to take to secure a virtual server environment?

Hands-On Projects

1. Read about virtualization security.

   ▪ Navigate to Chapter 8 of the Student Resource Center.
   ▪ Open Day2Session-VirtualizationSecurity-RickClaus.pdf and read the content.

2. Read about the security challenges in virtualized environments.

   ▪ Navigate to Chapter 8 of the Student Resource Center.
   ▪ Open Security Challenges in Virtualized Enviroments.pdf and read the content.

3. Read about virtualization security features.

   ▪ Navigate to Chapter 8 of the Student Resource Center.
   ▪ Open Virtualization_Security_Features.pdf and read the content.

Index

A

Application virtualization, 1-8–1-9

B

Business continuity
  Citrix XenApp, 4-9
  Hyper-V and, 3-4
  VMware and, 2-2, 2-3, 2-4, 2-5

C

Citrix, 1-16
Citrix XenApp business continuity, 4-9
Citrix XenServer 5, 4-2–4-6
Citrix Xen Virtualization, introduction, 4-1
Cloud computing, 1-13, 2-9
Clustering, 1-11

D

Desktop virtualization, 1-5, 1-6
Disconnected mode architecture, 5-5

E

Enterprise controller, 5-4

F

Full virtualization, 1-9, 6-2

G

Golden images, 8-3
Grid computing, 1-12

H

Hosted and bare-metal virtualization, 1-10
HP Virtual Server Environment, 1-17
Hyper-V
  architecture, 3-3, 3-4
  in business continuity and disaster recovery, 3-4
  creating virtual networks, 3-12, 3-13
  installation and configurations, 3-5–3-15
  key features of, 3-2–3-3
  security best practices, 3-15–3-16
  security prior–installation, 3-4–3-5
  security tips for, 3-15
  technology, 3-3
Hypervisor, defined, 3-3

M

Microsoft Virtualization
  with Hyper-V, 3-2–3-16. *See also* Hyper-V
  introduction, 3-1, 3-2
  overview, 1-15, 1-16
Migration, 1-11

N

Network virtualization, 1-8
NoMachine
  defined, 7-1
  introduction, 7-1–7-2
  NX server, 7-3–7-12
  NX technology, 7-2, 7-3
  overview, 1-17–1-18
NX technology, 7-2, 7-3

P

Parallels, for virtualization, 1-18
Paravirtualization, 1-10, 6-2
Partitioning, 1-10
Proxy controller, 5-4

R

Red Hat Enterprise Linux Virtualization
  basics, 6-1–6-3
  configuration, 6-7–6-10
  installation, 6-3–6-4
  installing guest operating systems, 6-4–6-7
  introduction, 6-1
  overview, 1-17
Role-based access control, 3-15

S

Server sprawl, 1-7
Server virtualization, 1-6–1-7

Software as a service (SaaS), 1-12–1-13
Standalone hosts, 2-11
Storage virtualization, 1-7
Sun virtualization
  desktops, 5-3, 5-4
  features of, 5-2–5-3
  introduction, 5-1–5-2
  product overview, 1-16–1-17
  security concerns with, 5-20
  Sun Virtual Desktop Infrastructure (VDI) software, 5-20, 5-21
  Sun xVM Ops Center, 5-4–5-18
  Sun xVM VirtualBox, 5-18–5-19, 5-20
Sun xVM Ops Center
  architecture, 5-4–5-5
  backup and recovery, 5-16
  enterprise controller, 5-7, 5-9–5-10, 5-16
  installation and configuration, 5-7–5-14
  introduction, 5-4
  port requirements, 5-5, 5-6
  proxy controller, 5-14–5-16
  updating, 5-12
  user and role management, 5-17–5-18
Sun xVM VirtualBox, 5-18–5-19, 5-20

V

virt-manager, 6-4
Virtual Iron, 1-17
Virtualization
  costs of, 8-3, 8-4
  defined, 1-2, 3-1, 5-1
  disaster recovery through, 1-14
  introduction, 1-2–1-3
  issues, 8-2–8-3
  security issues, 1-13–1-14
  techniques, 1-9–1-13
  types of, 1-5–1-9
  uses, 1-4
  vendors, 1-14–1-18

Virtualization security

benefits, 8-1–8-2

checklist, 8-4

introduction, 8-1

Virtualization stack, defined, 3-3, 4-3

Virtual machine, defined, 2-1

Virtual server product comparison, 4-2

VMware

business continuity and, 2-2, 2-3, 2-4, 2-5

disaster recovery and, 2-2–2-4, 2-5

overview, 1-15, 1-16

VMware Consolidated Backup, 2-12

VMware ESX, 2-4–2-9

VMware ESXi on Linux, introduction, 2-1, 2-2

VMware ESX Server systems

architecture of, 2-6

security for, 2-15–2-16

VMware vCenter Server, 2-13–2-15

VMware vSphere, 2-9–2-12, 2-13

X

X11 (or X) protocol, 7-2

X client, 7-2, 7-3

XenCenter, 4-7

Xen security, 4-7–4-9

X server, 7-2, 7-3

Y

yum command, 6-3